ARCHITECTURAL CARVING

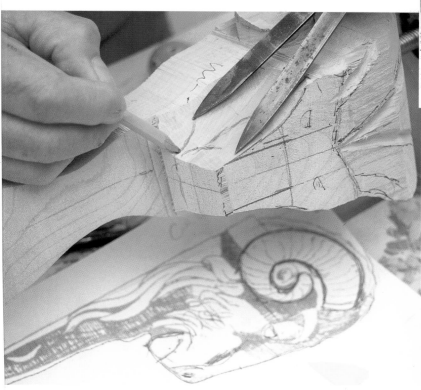

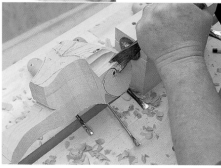

Techniques for Power & Hand Tools

Mike Burton

Sterling Publishing Co., Inc.
New York

DISCLAIMER

The author has made every attempt to present safe and sound carving practices, but he makes no claim that the information in this book is complete. The publisher and author can accept no legal responsibility for any consequences arising from the application of information, advice, or instructions given in this publication. The publisher shall not be liable for any special, consequential, or exemplary damage resulting, in whole or part, from the reader's use of, or reliance upon, this material.

Library of Congress Cataloging-in-Publication Data Available

Book design and layout by Judy Morgan

Edited by Rodman Pilgrim Neumann

2 4 6 8 10 9 7 5 3 1

Published by Sterling Publishing Co., Inc.
387 Park Avenue South, New York, NY 10016
© 2002 by Mike Burton
Distributed in Canada by Sterling Publishing
$^{c}/_{o}$ Canadian Manda Group, One Atlantic Avenue, Suite 105
Toronto, Ontario, Canada M6K 3E7
Distributed in Great Britain by Chrysalis Books
64 Brewery Road, London N7 9NT, England
Distributed in Australia by Capricorn Link (Australia) Pty. Ltd.
P.O. Box 704, Windsor, NSW 2756, Australia

Printed in China
All rights reserved

Sterling ISBN 1-4027-1384-3

To Carole, my wife of 39 years,
mother of my children/love of my life,
without whose support this book could not have been written.

And in memory of my mother Louise,
who left this world before the work could be completed.

With a special thanks to my son Benjamin Francis Burton
for his help with the drawings.

CONTENTS

INTRODUCTION — 6

PART I

WOODCARVING TOOLS, MATERIALS & EQUIPMENT — 10

1 THE WOODCARVING STUDIO & ITS FIXTURES — 12
Holding Fixtures ▪ A Woodcarver's Bench

2 ESSENTIAL WOODCARVING HAND TOOLS — 22
Chisels, Gouges, etc. ▪ Specialty Tools ▪ Acquiring Carving Tools ▪ Numbering ▪ Handles ▪ Knives ▪ Texturing Tools ▪ Mallets ▪ Rasps, Rifflers & So Forth ▪ Sanding Devices ▪ Measuring Devices ▪ Handy to Have

3 USEFUL POWER TOOLS — 43
Band Saws ▪ Routers ▪ Burrs & Tools to Drive Them ▪ Electrically Powered Chisels ▪ Pneumatically Powered Chisels ▪ Angle Grinders ▪ Power Sanders

4 SHARPENING WOODCARVING TOOLS — 59
Factors That Affect Tool Sharpness ▪ Bevels & Cutting Angles ▪ Testing for Sharpness ▪ Tool Shape ▪ Stones & Other Sharpening Devices ▪ Sharpening a New V Tool ▪ Sharpening Steel Rasps, Rifflers, Files & Burrs ▪ Power Sharpening

5 WOODS FOR CARVING — 75
Hardwoods ▪ Softwoods ▪ Notes on Gluing

PART II

LAYOUT, CARVING & FINISHING TECHNIQUES — 82

6 WORKING WITH PATTERNS, PHOTOGRAPHY & MODELS — 84
Working with Patterns ▪ Working with Photography ▪ Working with Models

7 LAYOUT OF SPECIAL SHAPES — 88
Polygons ▪ Ovals ▪ Spirals & Volutes ▪ Spiral Reeds

8 SAFETY PRECAUTIONS FOR WOODCARVERS — 97
Safety ▪ Hand Position

9 INCISED CARVING — 101
Chip Carving ▪ Triangular Designs ▪ Designs with Curves ▪ A Stylized Sunflower

10 RELIEF CARVING 113
Applied Carving

11 CARVING IN THE ROUND 122
Carving Spiral Reeds ▪ Holding the Form

12 FINISHING FOR MAXIMUM EFFECT 127
Preparation ▪ Patching ▪ Sanding ▪ Staining ▪ Topcoats ▪ Glaze ▪ Strikeout ▪
A Combination of Glaze & Strikeout

PART III
ARCHITECTURAL CARVING WITH POWER & HAND TOOLS 134

13 SET OF TOWEL BARS PROJECT 136
Layout ▪ Parting the Twist ▪ Carving the Twist ▪ Carving the Leaf ▪ Carving the Bar ▪
Preparing the Plugs

14 SPIRAL SHELF SUPPORTS PROJECT 145
Layout & Preliminary Steps

15 PAIR OF CARVED PANELS PROJECT 149
Developing the Pattern ▪ Setting-In the Design ▪ Patching ▪ Cleaning Up What the Router
Left ▪ Working the Stems ▪ Working the Leaves ▪ Working the Flowers & Buds ▪ Texturing
the Ground

16 PAIR OF COLUMN CAPITALS PROJECT 160
Initial Work ▪ Working with the Patterns ▪ Setting In the Volute & Shaping the Blank

17 DOOR WITH CARVED PANELS PROJECT 171
Preparing the Sash ▪ Preparing the Panels

18 UNUSUAL DOOR CASING PROJECT 185
The Faces ▪ The Plinth Blocks ▪ The Casing

PART IV
USEFUL TOOLS & EQUIPMENT YOU CAN BUILD 196

19 POWER STROP & SHARPENING STATION 198
The Base ▪ The Strop Wheel ▪ An Additional Accessory ▪ The Machine in Use

20 HOLDING FIXTURES 206
For Boards & Planks on Edge ▪ For Panels ▪ For Miscellaneous

21 ROTATING DEVICES 211
A Rotating Vise ▪ A Deluxe Rotating Vise ▪ Another Rotating Device

---

METRIC EQUIVALENTS 218

INDEX 220

INTRODUCTION

One would think that in these days of composition, injection molding, and even robots, there is no place for the individual carver. While manufactured embellishments are used most frequently, there are those clients that want something different, perhaps something more contemporary or just something that won't be seen anywhere else. There are those who simply prefer the "mark of the man's hand" to the perfection of the machine.

Clients who seek the work of the individual carver may be few, but there are enough of them to keep one busy executing commissioned works. Carving architectural embellishments is not something that someone usually does as a hobby. You could set out to decorate your own home or office, but usually you will find yourself working professionally for others, doing a very wide variety of work. Consequently, I have written this book with the efficiency achieved by the professional. Even if you are working for yourself and for pleasure, there is no reason you should take a week to do a day's work. That week is likely to be filled with frustration as well as pleasure.

Some of my shortcuts in technique and tooling might seem to encourage inferior work. I hope you don't get that impression, but I have never considered doing masterpiece work on a set of brackets that will wind up 16 feet from the floor. And if the unseeable top of the brackets is not finely detailed, so be it. I don't work to please the painter or cleaning crew.

I have a carved picture frame that has found some place on my desk for years. Until I started writing this book, I never looked closely at that frame. From a very critical view, the work is terrible. But when I look in that direction, my eye is drawn to the picture it encircles, my love of '62 who became my bride of '63. Such it is with most architectural carving. Remember that your work will not find its way to a contest as would the work of a fish or bird carver, to be viewed by knowing judges. For the most part, your work will be evaluated by those viewing the overall, not the minute, details. And your

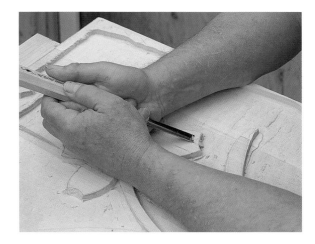

work should display the "mark of the man's hand," not the perfection of the machine.

There are those who take a very puritanical approach to woodcarving; only certain tools and techniques can be used. I was once one of them. When I found my pocketbook suffering, my attitude changed. In the following you'll find that I get the job done with any tool and technique that satisfies me. I'm no longer out to impress anyone with my technique, only the finished product.

You'll also note that I take a pragmatic approach to tooling at the expense of beauty

and form. In the following photos you'll see tools that are downright ugly, that exhibit rounded corners and poor polish, and that are generally in poor shape. My attitude is "if it ain't broke, don't fix it." I'm into carving, not tool display.

I consider myself a craftsman, a mechanic, by no means an artist or designer. That gets me out of a lot of design work that goes nowhere. As a result, I find myself working for architects and designers. I'm always willing to let them run the risk of the finished product not satisfying the client. The only problem here is that so many times I never get to see the finished product installed. Architects and designers tend to be very secretive as to their sources of supply and the destination of the finished product. As such, there are a couple of projects that I could not provide finished-product shots for this book.

As I consider tooling so very important, I have devoted considerable space to the subject. For the presentation I did considerable research, for it was not my intention to repeat the work of others. I have set forth some ideas that have had little or no exposure. Some may seem a bit radical, but I feel that all have merit.

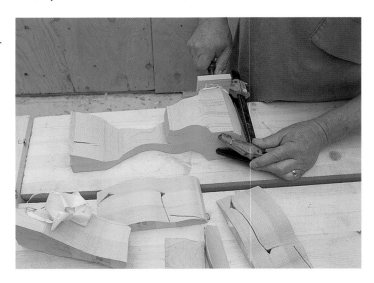

Architectural Carving: Techniques for Power & Hand Tools

They are geared to efficiency, not a puritanical approach to the craft.

Architectural carvers find themselves doing a wide variety of work. Through the techniques section and through the projects I have attempted to demonstrate that variety while again trying not to repeat other works. Over the past 30 years I have noticed a change in embellishments. Whereas most carving was once strictly traditional, there has been a shift to adaptations of traditional or downright contemporary designs. This is why you'll find no descriptions of the acanthus leaf in this book. While it is lovely and flowing, I've carved few in the last several years. I think that there is a trend for clients to express themselves through their decorating at the expense of tradition—sometimes at the expense of good taste. I can't count the times I've heard "Well, yes, that's fine, but it'll look like everybody else's."

The projects section is important in allowing you to follow in detail the steps taken to produce each piece. I don't furnish patterns and drawings but rather show how to develop your own pieces, how to adapt to your own dimensions and style. Scattered through each project there are techniques and tips that can't be found elsewhere. I felt it better to demonstrate these in a practical sense. Read and enjoy.

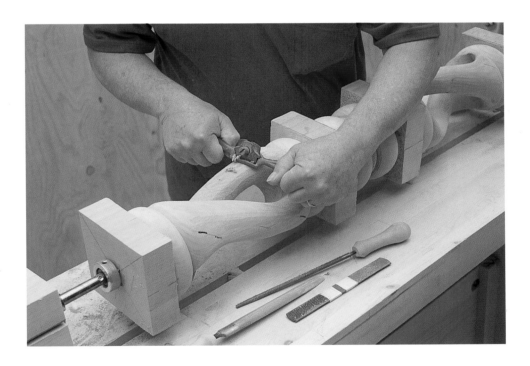

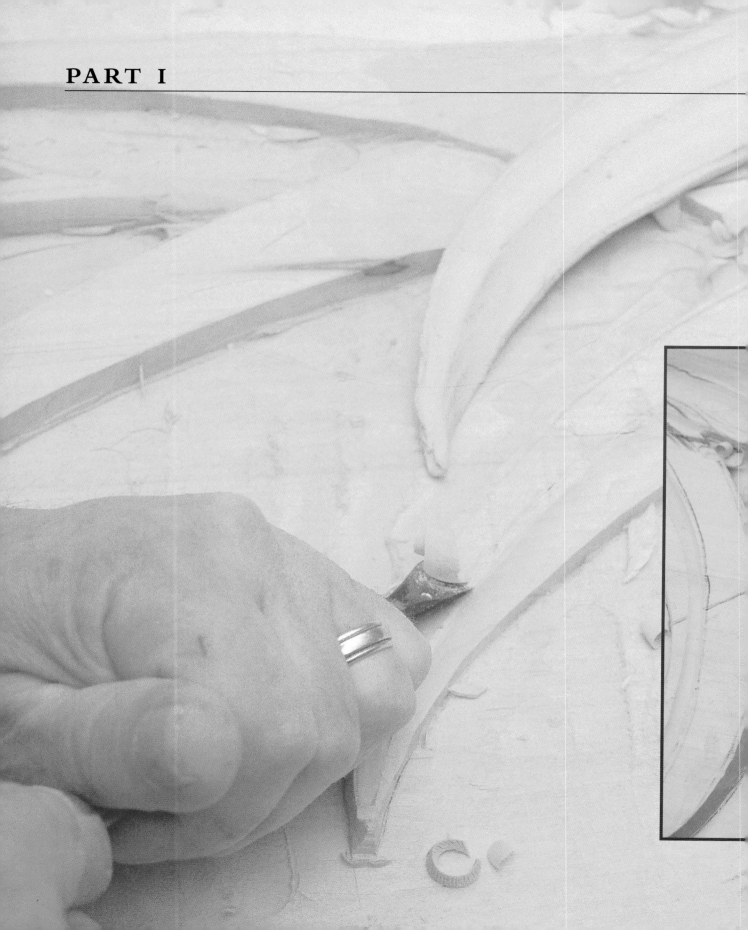

PART I

WOODCARVING TOOLS, MATERIALS & EQUIPMENT

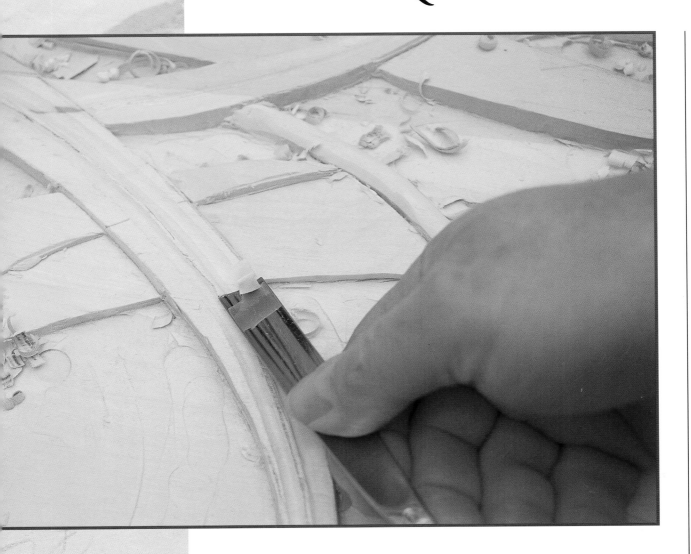

THE WOODCARVING STUDIO & ITS FIXTURES

I love the simplicity of woodworking. So much can be done with just a few simple tools. Architectural carving is not simple woodworking. To do the work efficiently you will need more than a chisel, a couple of gouges, and a rusty pocketknife. You will be confronted with a wide variety of projects—many needing special tooling. Some of the projects will require some heavy-duty tooling, whereas others will require very light, delicate tooling.

I refer to the place that I work in as a "studio." The people I do business with are clients. The terms stem from a meeting I had with my sons and partners many years ago. Cash flow was slow. Rather than increase production and lower prices, hoping to make up the difference in volume, we decided to upgrade our product and customers. The meeting produced a change in attitude and terminology. We determined that people who work in "studios" make more money than those who work in shops with less effort. Also, "clients" were easier to deal with and more affluent than customers, even though they were more discriminating and required a better product. Thus, the two words evolved. I do not know whether the words alone did any good but the change in attitude surely did.

Here I'm going to describe my studio and how to make your own workbench to suit your needs. In the following chapters I will discuss the tools I have in my studio in more detail and then again as I use them in the projects.

When you set up a studio for carving there are three words to remember: efficiency, efficiency, and, of course, efficiency. I moved into my present studio from a 7000-square-foot production facility that now belongs to my sons. I had a 1500-square-foot corner all to myself. My present studio is 240 square feet. Most of the photos in this book were taken in an area of 8 feet × 12 feet. Do I feel cramped? Not at all. In fact, my present studio is far more convenient.

I lined the walls with plywood so that I could fasten hangers and fixtures anywhere I wanted. My carving tools hang two deep on such a fixture (1-1). I found that

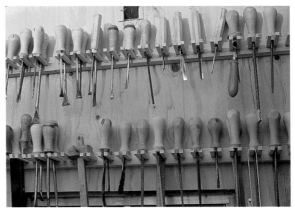

1-1 For convenience, tools can be hung on pegs surrounding the work area.

square pegs work best for most of my handles, but then I had access to a mortising machine to bore the square holes. It did save the cost of a lot of dowels.

I found that lightweight power tools can be hung by the cord over pegs screwed to the wall (1-2) (don't hang cords on screws or nails—in time the screw will cut through the cord). It's much better than having them on a shelf or in a drawer. Shelves and drawers seem to collect so

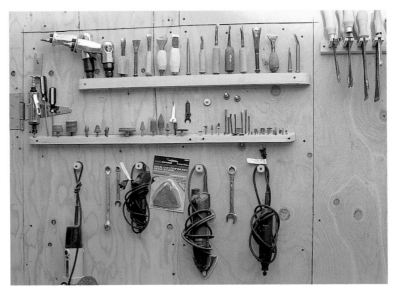

1-2 Lightweight power tools can be hung by their cords on pegs sufficiently large to prevent the cords from kinking.

much "stuff" for which they were not intended.

Also on the wall I hung specific wrenches to adjust my bench and various fixtures. It is so much nicer to have a proper-fitting wrench for adjustments rather than a pair of pliers or an adjustable wrench.

There are still a few tools stored in my tool cabinet, but with this arrangement I have the bulk of my arsenal at my fingertips and in plain view. It's so much nicer than digging through drawers for a tool.

There are a number of benches meeting the simple criteria in the sidebar—save for the height adjustment—that you can buy. I built my own, as detailed below, but for many years I worked on a bench similar to those that were built around the turn of the century. I stopped by my son's shop and snapped a photo of my old bench just for your viewing pleasure (1–3). For most projects, it was certainly adequate, but I often found myself blocking it up with

CRITERIA FOR A WORKBENCH

For most of the work you do as a carver you will want a good sturdy workbench. As you will be using carving tools along with a mallet, it should have little give in its surface, and it should have sufficient bulk that it won't move across the floor as force is exerted from the sides or ends. As I carve a wide variety of sizes and shapes for my projects, my bench is also adjustable in height.

Your workbench must be equipped with a means of holding the work being carved. This could be a vise or a number of different kinds of vise. Some benches have a number of holes drilled in them to accept pins that the vises can exert pressure against as they clamp against the work. All good benches should hang over their supporting frame far enough that clamps can be used to hold various projects to the surface.

14

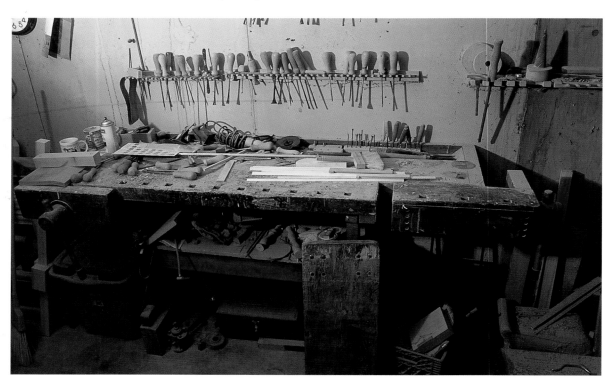

1-3 My old workbench, now in my son's shop.

pieces of 3×6 to bring it to the proper height; my arthritic back has an aversion to bending. You can see the blocks, probably left over from my last project there over seven years ago. Sometimes I found myself standing on those pieces of 3×6 to reach the work.

To keep from looking like a fool—standing on pieces of 3×6 and such—as the photos for this book were taken, I built the bench that I've always wanted but could never seem to find the time to build. See "A Woodcarver's Bench" below for all the details.

Another important detail is lighting. I like to see every nook and cranny of the piece I'm working on. The rafters and slanted roof of my work area are painted white to reflect all light downward. I have no dark spots and only light shadows. To evaluate the effects of shadow, I have the lighting on each wall on a separate switch. By manipulating the switches, I can cast many variations of shadow. For very critical shadows and showing defects, I keep a flashlight handy. This may seem a bit unconventional, but I have never been troubled with headaches from

LIGHTING CONSIDERATIONS

If you can set up your work area under a skylight, that's wonderful. I have but one small window in my studio, but the work area is encircled with fluorescent lights. Many carvers advise working with incandescent cross lighting to get a more distinct shadow. When using incandescent lights, place them in such a manner that they bring out the shadows of the carving in the work.

To eliminate the flicker of the florescent lighting—or at least double its speed—I have connected alternate fixtures to opposite sides of the 220-volt line.

fluorescent lighting and don't find the indistinct shadows to be any bother.

Above all, keep your studio convenient. If you find that you need a simple fixture, such as a tray to hold burrs you are using, take a few minutes to build it **(1–4)**. Keep your work area pleasant and agreeable. And always remember: The only difference between work and play is your attitude.

15

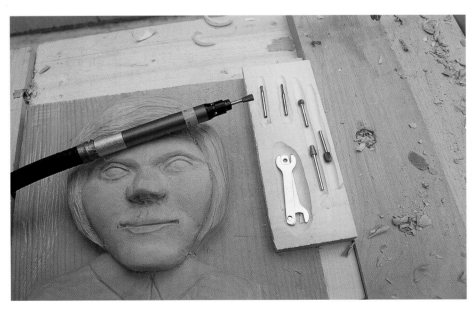

1-4 As work progresses, simple fixtures can be contrived for special purposes.

HOLDING FIXTURES

In addition to vises, benches might be equipped with a number of different kinds of fixtures to hold the work. These may be simple spring-shank dogs or "holdfasts" that can be driven into holes in the bench to hold the work down **(1-5)**. There are also toggle clamps **(1-6)**. These do hold the work in place but must be fastened to the bench. Anything bolted in one place is too restrictive for me. It's always in the wrong place.

Another item is a screw that can be passed through a hole in the bench and threaded into the base of the work **(1-7)**—great for

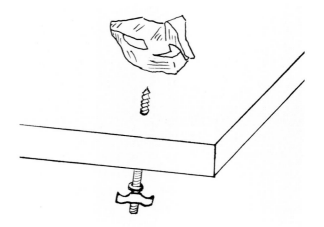

1-7 A bench screw.

doing a bust or a lion's head. As I do very few busts or lions' heads, I've never invested in one of these special screws. I find a lag bolt works very well on the few occasions I've had to use such a fixture.

If you intend to do any carving in the round, I highly recommend a rotating vise to hold the work. Look at the one in Chapter 21, "Rotating Devices," in the section on "Useful Tools & Equipment You Can Build," for some ideas.

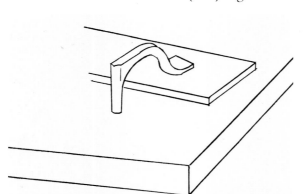

1-5 A holdfast.

A WOOD-CARVER'S BENCH

Take a look again at the photo above (*see* **1-4**) of the bench I used for many years. Each time I worked on that bench I made mental notes of its shortcomings and ways to overcome them. The first thing was the height. It made no difference what type of project I worked; the bench was either too high or too low to accommodate my arthritic back.

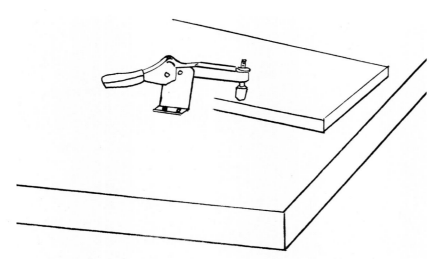

1-6 A toggle clamp.

16

The other serious drawback was the tool tray. It prevented me from working on either side of the bench, so I was forever turning the work. Besides, that tray always filled with chips. Small tools got lost in the chips and, when I swept the chips onto the floor, the tools went with them—falling on their cutting edge, of course. The tray had to go.

I did enjoy the vises, but I just had this idea that I could do better, or at least as well, for holding fixtures.

I also enjoyed the stout top that was about 2½ inches thick. The only problem there is that it was glued up from only two planks and it was cupped slightly. When working on a large panel, that cup was a pain in the posterior.

My criteria for a new bench were quite simple: height adjustable, no tray, not wider than necessary so that I could work from both sides, and it had to have a stout, stable top. I also gave some thought to holding fixtures. I wanted the new fixtures to operate from the center of the bench for most work. Moving the tailstock back and forth on my lathe gave me some inspiration, but I noticed that it had to be drawn down quite tight to keep it from moving. Would this withstand the blows of a mallet or air chisel? I came up with the idea of using a dovetailed slot to hold a dovetailed block. Experimentation showed that with the block pulled down only slightly, there was no movement—one addition to the list of criteria.

I've built several smaller prototypes of the bench I'm about to describe but I think this will be the last. I think I've finally run out of ideas to incorporate or things to simplify.

Material Preparation

Now I wouldn't want you to get the idea that I'm overly thrifty, but I am. I could see no reason to assemble the bench top from expensive hardwood. I chose the cheapest,

yet decent, wood I could think of—eight-foot lumberyard 2 × 4s. These are a price item and dealers want to have the cheapest in town. I did buy a few extras, because I knew that there were bound to be a couple of rejects.

I did select the 2 × 4s. Of course, I picked them for being "reasonably straight," but before I looked to see if they were straight, I looked at the ends. I didn't want any "boxed heart." That is, I didn't want to see the center of the tree in any of them. I was reasonably successful, but you'll see a heart in the glued-up assembly in **1-8** below.

1-8 A piece of maple is glued between the assemblies of the bench top.

Lumberyard stock is kiln-dried. The stock I bought had "S dry" stamped on it. I think the "S" stands for "sorta." Lumberyard stock is dried to about 20-percent moisture content, and that is far too wet for a stable bench top. In addition, lumberyard stock might not be consistent. There might be some at 20 percent, some at 12 percent, and some at 25 percent. This would not do.

The first step then was to put the stock on stickers in my "solar dry kiln" (1-9). This kiln consists of a pair of horses to keep the stock off the ground. I cover this with a piece of black plastic film and put a fan—on slow speed—under the pile to circulate the air gently. With

1-9 Stock is stickered and placed in a solar dry kiln.

worked carefully but made no special effort to bend any into shape.

Once the glue was dry, I took the glue-ups to the mill and faced one side and edge, then ran them through the planer until all evidence of the eased edge of the 2 × 4s was gone. This yielded two blanks that were 3 inches thick and about 7½ inches wide. At the mill I glued a piece of 8/4 soft maple between them.

Then I ripped this assembly at center and at a 15-degree angle. After a couple of passes over the jointer each half had the angle plus a ¾-inch square spot. I've shaded the soft maple in **1-8**. One of these halves will be rotated to provide for a bench top with a dovetailed slot down the center.

days above 90°F (32°C) this kiln will dry stock in less than a week.

The kiln's only drawback is wind. I live in the mouth of a canyon at the base of the Wasatch Mountains. The gale-force morning winds often send that plastic into the neighbor's backyard and scatter the bricks that I put on it to hold it down all over the driveway.

What is that blue thing under the left legs of the horse? That, gentle reader, is my moisture meter. It amounts to nothing more than a bathroom scale. When the pile quits losing weight, it's dry.

Preparing the Top

Once the 2 × 4s were dry, I cut them at 64 inches. For each one I cut, I was left with a 32-inch piece. These shorts I butted together as I glued up two stacks of five, face to face **(1-10)**. I

1-10 The stock is glued up five pieces thick.

Architectural Carving: Techniques for Power & Hand Tools

Preparing the Legs

Assembling the legs came next. The first of this type bench I built, I mortised the legs into a piece of 12/4-inch material. With this one I was lazy. I glued up three pieces of 4/4-inch material with the leg components sandwiched between them **(1-11)**. On the split member I placed a ¾-inch spacer loosely between the uprights to keep them spaced properly. Before glu-

ing up the other member, I fastened the ¾-inch guide stick to it, then again spread glue on all of the pieces and clamped them together **(1-12)**.

At no time did I pay any particular attention to the length of the pieces that made up the base and top, only that there was plenty of length. After the glue was dry, I took each to the band saw and cut it to exact length and shape. I also cut out a notch in which to fasten a foot **(1-13)**.

1-11 The leg components are sandwiched between three layers of 4/4 material.

19

1-12 The guide stick is fastened before gluing.

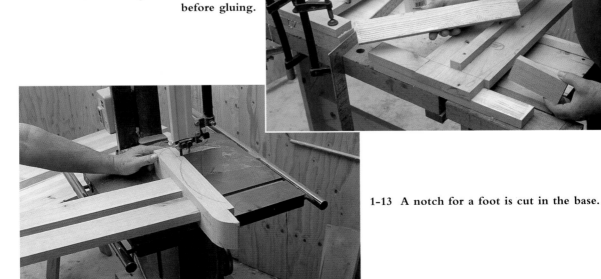

1-13 A notch for a foot is cut in the base.

BUYING WOOD

Note that wood is still sold in "quarters" based on the rough-cut dimension before surfacing, so that 8/4, or 2 inches, is really equal to an actual thickness of 1¾ inches after planing, the same way a 2 × 4 is not really 2 inches by 4 inches.

The Center Support

After gluing strengthening sticks to both sides of the ends of the plywood center support, I drilled the necessary holes and squared the edge next to the stick so that a washer would lie flat against it (1-14).

Final Assembly

I've set out the components in their position of assembly in 1-15. You will note some pieces of brown wrapping paper. In operation a dovetailed stick will slide down the slot in the center of the bench to secure various hold-down fixtures. This stick will tend to push the halves apart. It was my original intention to glue the supports to the bench top. Then I said to myself, "Self, what if you want to take it apart for some reason?" That's when I decided to put a piece of paper in the glue line. The glued paper will hold sufficiently, but if I ever want to take the bench apart, a chisel will part the paper. Once the paper was glued in place I inserted the lag bolts in predrilled holes. If you don't have an impact wrench for that little operation, I suggest borrowing or renting one (1-16).

1-14 One side of the hole is squared to accommodate a washer.

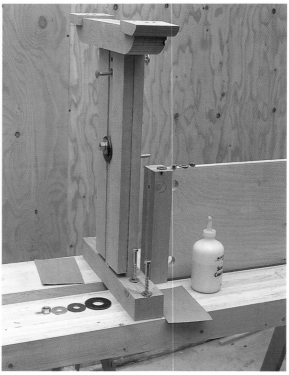

1-15 The position of the various components.

Architectural Carving: Techniques for Power & Hand Tools

1-16 An impact wrench is the best way to install the lag screws.

The Woodcarving Studio & Its Fixtures

ESSENTIAL WOODCARVING HAND TOOLS

If it seems that architectural carving requires a large investment in tools, keep in mind that I've collected tools over a period of 40-odd years and I did a lot of work without all of the tools I have now. Each time I found a tool that would add to my efficiency and a particular project would bear its cost, I bought it. Some tools were gifts, some were purchased at pawn shops or yard sales. I suggest you add to your tooling in the same manner.

CHISELS, GOUGES, ETC.

Traditional woodcarving is done with chisels (**2-1,** left). A chisel with its cutting edge not ground perpendicular to the axis of its shaft is called a "skew" (**2-1,** second left). There are also curved chisels called "gouges" (**2-1,** second right). Tools that make a V-shaped cut are called "parting tools" or "veiners." And there is a tool that is shaped like a U with a flat bottom, called a macaroni tool. It has a bevel on all three sides. If I had a macaroni tool, I would

2-1 **Woodcarving chisels.**

have snapped a picture of it for you, but in all of my years of carving, I've never found use for one. All of these tools come in a wide variety of widths and, in the case of gouges, the radius of the curve or "sweep" can vary from $\frac{1}{32}$ inch to several inches (**2-2**).

2-2 **Woodcarving gouges of varying sweep.**

The bevel of gouges is usually formed on the outside of the body of the tool, but it might be formed in the channel of the gouge. These are called "in channel." The tools may have straight or slightly tapered bodies (**2-3,** left), or they may flair out at the cutting edge like the tail of a fish (**2-3,** right). Would you believe that these are called "fishtail" tools? These are superb tools for getting into tight places. Most of my tools are fishtails, but that is an accident of manufacture rather than intentional.

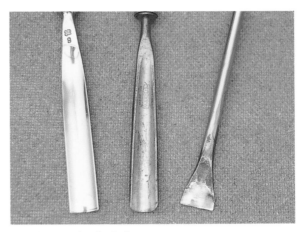

2-3 **Gouge-shank design.**

All tools may be bent slightly forward, called "fore-bent" tools (**2-4,** left). These are very handy for tight places where a higher angle of attack is necessary (**2-5**).

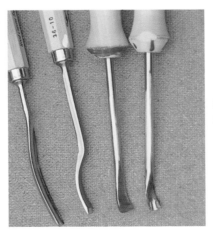

2-4 **Bent gouges.**

23

2-5 Fore-bent gouges facilitate a higher angle of attack.

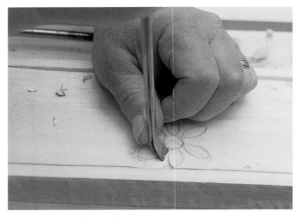

2-7 The shank of tightly fore-bent gouges are usually pushed with the thumb.

Tools may also be bent backward, called "back-bent" (**2-4,** second left). I find these especially useful for cutting beads (**2-6**).

Gouges might be bent very tightly near the cutting edge; these are called "spoons" (**2-4,** right). I even have a few chisels that are tightly fore-bent (**2-4,** second right). These are especially useful in tight places. They are usually held by the handle but pushed with the thumb of the other hand (**2-7**).

And some tools, especially chisels, can have a kink in the body; these are referred to as "doglegs" (**2-8A** and **B**). These are somewhat similar to the fore- and back-bent tools, but the area between the cutting edge and kink is flat. Doglegs can be used somewhat like a tiny

2-8A Using a dogleg tool.

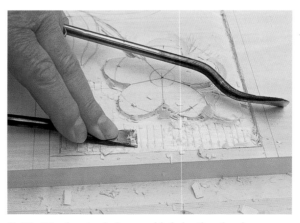

2-8B Dogleg tools have a kink in the shank.

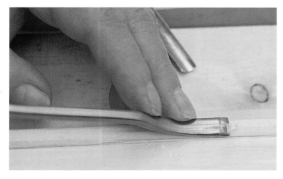

2-6 Back-bent gouges work well for rounding off beads.

plane when the flat area is held tightly against the work.

I must add that since I acquired a couple of power die grinders and a good selection of burrs, a lot of my "tight place" tools get little use.

SPECIALTY TOOLS

For very tight places, bent skews **(2-9)** are handy to have. These, of course, come in pairs, one right-handed and one left-handed.

2-9   Skews can also be bent.

I have another close-quarters tool that I have not seen on the market but that comes in very handy for cleanup. It is actually a sharp screwdriver. Working in another's shop, I was carving a design that had a lot of sharp intersections, much the same as those I encountered in the floral panel project **(2-10)**, detailed in Chapter 7. My bent skews were not quite right for the job, but the boss had a brand new set of inexpensive screwdrivers. One is now missing from that set. With the aid of a grinder and small stone I formed it into that slightly bent, double-sided "skew" **(2-11)**. Yes, I did buy the boss a new set of cheap screwdrivers before I left his employ.

A very handy tool is the skewed gouge. There will be times when you want to leave a

2-10   There are situations that defy conventional tools.

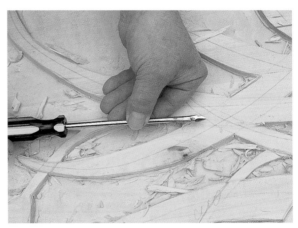

2-11   Special-purpose tools can be formed from such things as a screwdriver.

sharp, delicate ridge between two concave elements of a design. Shells and fans come immediately to mind. If these elements run diagonally across the grain, the gouge you're using to hollow them will be cutting with the grain on one side and against the grain on the other. This tends to tear out that delicate ridge. You could tip a standard gouge so that it cuts more with the grain, but that can be awkward. With a skewed gouge, even though you are pushing the tool against the grain, it will be cutting from top to bottom and essentially with the grain **(2-12)**.

25

2-12 Skewed gouges can cut against the grain.

2-13A Using a veneer saw.

For making long, straight parting cuts, a saw with a curved blade comes in very handy. If you have a veneer saw, give it a try **(2-13)**. I have another device I rescued from the thrift store **(2-14)**. It is nothing more than a stainless-steel table knife with saw teeth filed in it using the serration as a guide. While you're at the thrift store, pick up a table knife without serration. They make excellent putty knives.

SKEWED GOUGES

Skewed gouges must be purchased in pairs—one right-handed and one left-handed. These are not items that I would run out and buy immediately, but I'd certainly put them on a wish list.

ACQUIRING CARVING TOOLS

Now, 'tis true that a large volume of varied work can be produced with a half-dozen tools—I've even seen some very impressive work produced with a rusty pocket knife—but for reasons of speed and neatness you will find yourself collecting quite an assortment of costly tools. I have many more than I need **(2-15)**. There are over 200 tools hanging on those walls. When I had to

2-13B A veneer saw works well for making straight parting cuts.

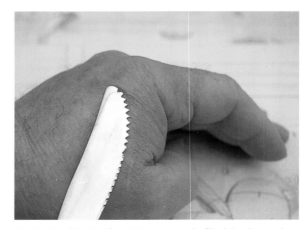

2-14 A table knife with saw teeth filed in; it works for straight parting cuts.

Architectural Carving: Techniques for Power & Hand Tools

26

2-15 You can acquire too many tools.

add the second row to the left, I also added the shelf below. All it does is collect junk, but it is a safety measure. A person walking too close to that wall could lose an ear.

I keep telling myself that someday I'm going the go through all of those tools and date them. Each time I use a tool, I'll update it. After three years, I will dispose of any tools

bearing the first dating. It's fun to think about, but I'll probably never get to it.

To mark special tools that I used frequently I put a piece of masking tape on the shank. It wasn't long before most of my tools had masking tape on the shank. Then I tried different colors of masking tape. Soon some tools had two and three colors of tape and frustration set in again.

THE EXPENSE OF TOOLS

Cost has never been a concern to me, as I make my own tools. I can produce the average serviceable gouge in about 15 minutes from less than fifty cent's worth of raw material. Yes, I'm thrifty—perhaps downright "cheap" is a better word—but I derive a great deal of satisfaction working with tools fashioned by my own hand.

Though I have tried to use store-bought tools in the photos of this book, I have few and some of my shop-mades have crept into the photos. Please forgive their appearance, for very often they still bear the marks of the hammer and fire whence they were wrought. I generally concern myself with a comfortable handle and ¼ inch of the cutting end. What falls between is irrelevant to me.

For those that will be laying out larger sums than I for tools, I have one piece of advice: DON'T run out and buy them all at once. Don't opt for that super humongous set of every tool you could ever want at the astonishing discount of 10 percent over the cost of purchasing them individually. Over half of those tools you will touch only once as you hang them on the wall or put them in the included canvas carrying case—a lot of my shop-made tools have only been used a couple of times. Rather, purchase a small starter set and build as needs and finances dictate.

27

NUMBERING

Enter my own numbering and marking system, stage left. Being unconcerned with the width of the tools, I measured the sweep on a cone I turned for the purpose (2-16). Then I assigned each tool a number relating to the diameter of the circle it would cut. The system worked in increments of ⅛ inch. A number-one tool will cut a circle of ⅛ inch, a number-two tool will cut a circle of ¼ inch, a number-12 tool will cut a circle of 12/8 inch or 1½ inches. The number is completely independent of the width of the tool and relates only to the diameter of the circle it will cut.

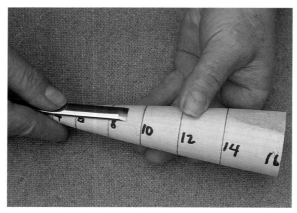

2-16 A tapered cone can be used to measure the sweep of gouges.

I then took the system to the max by marking each tool with a color code used by the electronics industry: 0 = black, 1 = brown, 2 = red, 3 = orange, 4 = yellow, 5 = green, 6 = blue, 7 = violet, 8 = gray, 9 = white. In the case of the number-two gouge mentioned above, it has a daub of red paint on it (2-18A, second right). In the case of the number 12, it has a daub of brown with a daub of red to the right (2-18A, third right).

Some of my gouges cut a very large circle four, five, six inches. These I marked with a band of paint to indicate the sweep as the shallow gouge in 2-18A, right.

TOOL CATALOGUE NUMBERS

Quality carving tools have a number stamped in the shank. The number relates to the type of tool and its width and dates to the 1880s when a regular list of tools being made was published. It became known as the Sheffield List, from the tool-making heart of England, and is a numerical description still widely used to identify carving tools. This numbering system works great for identifying the items in catalogues, but, especially in the case of gouges, it really doesn't help me at all. The three gouges in 2-17 are all stamped with the same sweep number. You will note that as the width of the tool decreases, so does the radius of cut. Often I will have several different sweeps of gouge on my bench and some with the same sweep but different widths. I can visually identify the width of the gouges quite easily, but I sometimes pick up several different tools trying for the right sweep. Needless to say this exercise was frustrating and wasted considerable time.

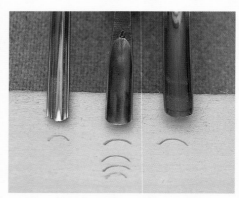

2-17 The sweep of gouges stamped with the same number can vary.

Chisels I marked with a broken black line (2-18A, left). Skews have dots of black (2-18A, second left), and V tools have a band of black (2-18A, third left).

With all of these wonderful color codes, I can easily identify a tool on the bench or

Architectural Carving: Techniques for Power & Hand Tools

return it quickly to its proper place on my tool hangers. Sometimes I will even make notes on the pattern I'm using as to what gouge to use where (2-18B).

While the foregoing may seem utterly ridiculous, it has saved me a great deal of frustration and wasted time. Since I work professionally, time is important, as time is money.

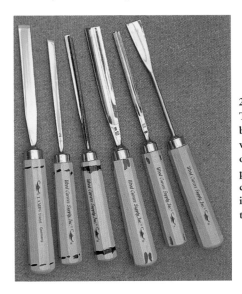

2-18A Tools can be marked with daubs of colored paint for quick identification.

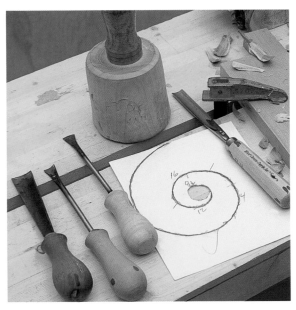

2-18B Notes can be made on a pattern, indicating which tool to use where.

HANDLES

In some parts of the world carvers do not have handles on their tools. I recently read an article describing a Balinese carver. His tools were merely long steel shanks formed on one end. These he either pushed by hand or struck with a small metal hammer similar to the type used by stone carvers. The arrangement didn't look overly comfortable. I think I'll stick to handled tools.

Fitted to the metal shank of Western tools there is usually a wooden handle. Today there are probably tools with plastic handles, but I don't think that I could force my hand around such a handle no matter its size or shape. Viewing the tools of a longtime carver, you might encounter a handle that appears to be a stick or a dowel, unceremoniously whittled for comfort (2-19, left). This was probably a handle quickly contrived to replace one that was broken through hard use.

More than likely the handles you will see will be slightly bulbous and about 4 inches in length and $7/8$ inch in diameter (2-19, fourth left). A variation of this handle will be octagonal (2-19, third left)—great for preventing narrow tools from rolling off of the bench.

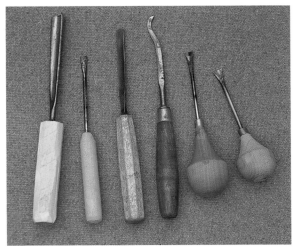

2-19 Carving tools can have many different kinds of handle.

Another type of handle is called the "doorknob" (2-19, first and second right). This is a great handle for pushing with the hand alone and is usually affixed to smaller tools for doing fine, detail work.

COMPONENTS OF CHISELS

You'll note that some of the tools have a shoulder on the shank as it fits to the handle. This is to prevent the shank being driven deeper into the handle. You'll also note that some of the tools have a metal ferrule where handle and shank meet. The shoulder is of some value, for the shanks of these tools are tapered and would tend to split the handle if driven too deep. (The handle I describe in the accompanying text requires no shoulder, as the bottom of the shank is flat. I've been using this system for years and the number of handles I've broken can be counted on one hand.) The ferrule makes for good engineering and a prettier tool, but it is unnecessary. Pressure that would damage a handle with no ferrule would come from prying with the tool. This should never be done, nor should a small carving tool be struck hard enough to damage the handle.

If it's heavy-duty tools you need, consider tools with a socket handle (2-20). These tools can be struck very hard without damaging the handle. I did have a couple of socket tools, but since I've had the air hammer, I let the power tool do my heavy-duty work.

I will present a slightly different handle for your consideration. When you are pushing a standard handle with the hand, the end digs into the heel of the hand at the entrance to the carpal tunnel (2-21)—the place where the nerves pass from the wrist into the hand. After long hours of carving my hands would often become numb. My doctor explained the probable cause of the numbness and advised me to take up other work.

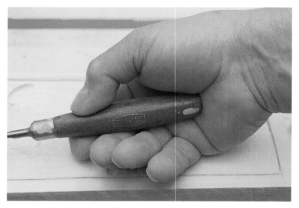

2-21 Pushing on the small handle of a carving tool with the heel of the hand can be dangerous.

"Bah, humbug," said I. Rather than give up work I love, I designed a new handle that I could easily turn from the abundance of rippings that always pile up around the studio (2-22). (You might want to adjust the length to fit your hand.) The larger diameter of the handle makes it easier for me to grip and control, while the bulbous end spreads the pressure over a greater area of the heel of the hand. In addition, that ridge toward the front of the handle permits me to push with the thumb and forefinger, taking even more pressure off of the heel of the hand (2-23). And when I am using the tool with a mallet, that ridge fits ever so comfortably into the palm of my hand (2-24).

The handle does have a fault. Small tools fitted to it tend to roll off onto the floor. This little challenge is easily met by sanding a few flat spots on it (2-24A). My fault is that I don't sand

2-20 A socket chisel.

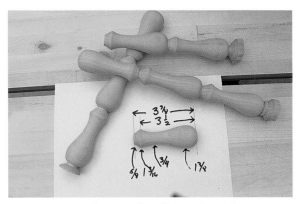

2-22 A larger diameter handle can be safer.

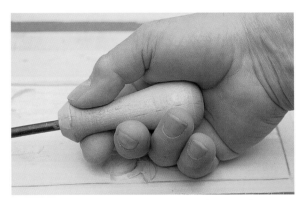

2-23 Pushing with thumb and forefinger relieves pressure on the heel of the hand.

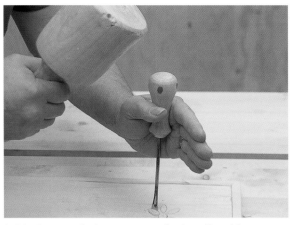

2-24 A second character on the handle adds to comfort when the tool is used with a mallet.

2-24A Flat spots can be cut on the handle to prevent tools from rolling onto the floor.

2-24B To bore handles for tapered shanks, tapered bits can be ground.

the flat spots until the tool has hit the floor a couple of times.

One little note: If you're fitting new handles to your tools you might want to grind a twist bit to fit the tapered shank (2–24B). Depending on the taper of your shank, you might even have to grind two and use them successively. You should not grind into the flutes of the bit when tapering it.

KNIVES

In addition to chisels, gouges, and the like, a carver should be equipped with a few knives. I don't have a large assortment, but the ones I do have serve me well.

When those around you find that you have taken up woodcarving, you might be presented with a set of hobby knives (2-25, left). It happened to me. I received a set of three handles along with a large assortment of disposable blades, all in their own carrying case. I did thank the gift-giver but have found little use for the knives. Yes, they are very sharp and good for very fine detail work, but I find that the blades are too flexible, thus hard to control. In most cases, you will find that plain old utility knife that you already have (2-25, third right) will be more satisfactory.

One knife I use quite frequently is a linoleum, or floor-covering, knife (2-25, right). This knife has two great features: the blade is stout enough that it doesn't flex, and the shape of the blade permits a clear view of the cut being made. I find it very handy for cleaning up "wood whiskers" around a set-in design, to say nothing of cutting out patterns and such. It's also great for finishing off a parting cut that wasn't quite deep enough (2-26).

Also borrowed from the floor covering industry is the carpet-pad knife (2-25, second right), a great little knife for whittling-type operations. I sometimes use mine as a putty

2-26 A floor-covering knife is especially handy.

knife, but I cleaned it off and polished it so that it could smile at you in the photo.

The three knives in the center of 2-25 are home brews that I use occasionally. One has a straight blade and the others are curved, one to the right and one to the left. These are great for getting into tight spots, and only the tip of the blade is usually used.

Gentle reader, I have a confession. When I reach for a knife, the first one I reach for is that

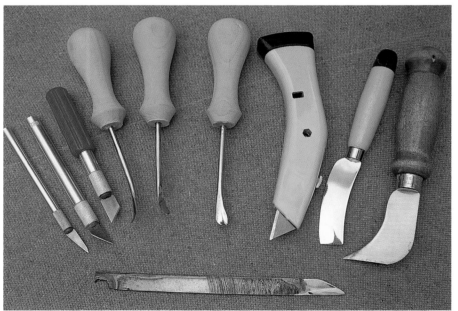

2-25 A collection of various knives is most useful.

32

ugly thing lurking in the bottom of **2–25**. It is nothing more than a strip of steel cut from an old saw blade with 1 inch of the end tempered and sharpened. It is stout, does not flex, is easy to control for light cuts, and stays razor sharp. It's the best knife I have for digging out slivers. Someday I may put some sort of handle on it, but for now . . .

TEXTURING TOOLS

Rather than cut, texturing tools emboss the wood. That is, they stamp a design shallowly into it. They are usually used to add texture to the background of a relief carving.

The first time I needed a texturing tool, I needed it "yesterday." There was no time for even overnight delivery. Undaunted, I grabbed an old bolt and a triangular file **(2–27)**. In fifteen minutes I had a texturing tool. The next time I needed a texturing tool, the first one I made I found to be too fine for the reproduction I was working, so I made another, and another, and another **(2–28)**. I do have quite a collection, but the next time I need to texture a background, I'll bet none of them fit, so it will be back to another bolt and file.

If you are working your own designs, you might find that a handful of nails held with a rubber band **(2–29)** will give you a suitable

2-28 **Texturing tools can be made in many different sizes.**

2-29 **Even a few nails can serve as a texturing tool.**

texture. If not, buying is certainly easier than making. You might even wish to consider leather-embossing tools. These will put a light texture in wood as well as leather.

MALLETS

Carving tools can be powered by hand pressure alone. But you'll find that when working in hard-textured woods, or making deep cuts in soft-textured woods, striking the end of the tool with something saves a lot of muscle. If woodcarving is part of your physical-fitness program, by all means forget striking the tool and push away.

You could strike the tool with the heel of your hand. I've even seen hand pads specifically designed for the practice, but I—and my doctor—would advise against it. The practice

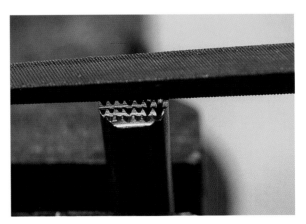

2-27 **Such things as texturing tools can be easily fabricated in the studio.**

33

is hard on the wrist, and in the heel of the hand is the entrance to the carpal tunnel, the passageway for the nerves to the hand.

Stone carvers strike their tools with a steel hammer, and I've seen some woodcarvers use a wooden hammer-like device (2-30). I cannot hit a carving tool with a hammer, although I do a pretty good job on that bone located where my thumb joins my hand. When I dabbled in stone carving, I used a 4-inch-long by 2½-inch-diameter pipe-nipple filled with lead. This I coupled to a short length of ¾-inch pipe for a handle. It worked great for me, and the folks in the class got a lot of laughs . . . till they tried it.

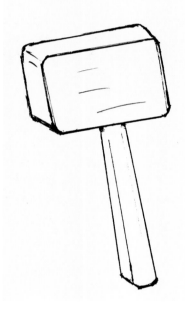

2-30 A carver's hammer.

Were I to buy a mallet, I would strongly consider one of those made from a firm rubber-like material. In lieu of that, I turn my own from poplar (2-31). I turn the handle separately and can often salvage it when the head becomes unusable. The soft poplar heads don't last forever, but I always have a good supply of poplar end cuts around the studio that can be glued up to turn mallet heads from.

MALLET SHAPE

I do my best work with a round wooden mallet. You will see these in all of the woodworking supply catalogues. If possible I would avoid the very hard and heavy types made of lignum vitae or hard maple. You shouldn't be striking a tool that heavily. If heft is what you require, consider the "air chisel" mentioned in Chapter 3, "Useful Power Tools." Besides, it has always been my feeling that the mallet should be no harder than the tool handles. I would rather replace one mallet than a number of tool handles.

2-31 Mallets and handles can be quickly turned from scraps.

RASPS, RIFFLERS & SO FORTH

I must confess, gentle reader, that for a time I took a puritanical approach to woodcarving. Nothing, and I mean nothing, was to touch the work except chisel, gouge, knife, and an occasional scraper. Such things as rasps, rifflers, and sandpaper were for sissies who could not skillfully use their chisels, gouges, etc. As I tried making a living carving, I was often asked to duplicate the work of others, fine detailed work with no obvious tool marks. My attitude changed. I found that the work could perhaps be done with chisels and gouges alone but it would take quite a wide assortment of those tools—an assortment beyond my budget at the

Architectural Carving: Techniques for Power & Hand Tools

time. Even with an awesome assortment of tools, I could see that there were places that needed the attention of something else. I could also see that there just might be a "something else" that could do a better job than chisels and gouges alone. Enter rasps and rifflers.

It is still my attitude that all the work that can be efficiently done with chisels and gouges should be done with these tools, for they remove material far more quickly than any other devices—save for some power tools. While rasps and rifflers are by no means a panacea, they can perform some tasks quite efficiently.

Rasps

Rasps come in many sizes, shapes, and forms (2-32). The rasp I usually reach for first is called a "shoe" or "horseshoe" rasp—the two on the left in 2-32. One side of the rasp is flat, the other curved. Each side has a coarse and fine section and it has no handle.

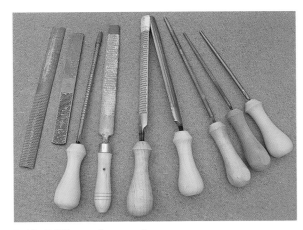

2-32 Different forms of rasp.

Third from the left rests a round rasp, great for tightly curved surfaces. Fourth, fifth, and sixth are gently curved on one side and flat on the other. The sixth is actually a coarse metal-working file, as are the three round devices to

the right. The metal-working tools work well to remove marks left by the coarse rasps.

You will note the masking tape on the ends of some of the devices. No, that's not so I can easily identify them. The tape is there to prevent them from removing more hide from my thumb than from the wood I'm working on. Rasps are usually held with both hands. Also, you will note that all of the devices capable of receiving a handle have one. Don't use a rasp without a handle. Eventually you will ram the tang into your hand—it's painful, and you could get blood on your work. Rather, ram the tang into a handle, even if it's a dowel or just a plain stick of wood.

Rifflers

Smaller rasps designed to get into tight places are called "rifflers." These come in a very wide variety of sizes and shapes (2-33). You would think that in that pile in 2-33 there would be any size or shape I could ever desire. Wrong. The two at the top were a couple that I made for some special project.

Smiling at you to the left in 2-33 is a wire brush. Rifflers clog quite easily. If you have no means to clean the riffler, you have only half a riffler. Use only a brass bristle brush to clean your rifflers; a steel brush will dull them

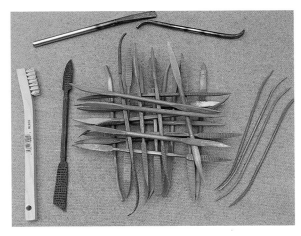

2-33 Rifflers.

quickly. If you are working in a very resinous wood it's also a good idea to have a can of strong solvent—MEK, acetone, even lacquer thinner—to soak the riffler, thereby softening the resin, before attempting any cleaning. Rifflers also come coarse and fine (2–34).

There is a riffler that doesn't bite: the diamond riffler (2–35). This steel tool is coated with chips of diamond. I'm told that the diamond chips are held in place through some electroplating process. These tools also come coarse and fine (2–36). The coarse ones are about the equivalent of 80-grit sandpaper, while the fine are the equivalent of 220-grit sandpaper. That's quite a spread, but it's a workable spread. The rifflers in 2–35 with the black handles are from a different manufacturer than the ones in the center and are the equivalent of about 120-grit sandpaper. I am, therefore, armed with a complete range.

The rifflers in the center of 2–35 did have one disadvantage: no handle. They were rather hard to control as the shank twisted easily in my hand. A few wire nuts met that little challenge.

When new, some diamond particles will come loose, so use the riffler on a scrap of wood first. Diamond particles can mess up the edge of a carving tool used to make a final cut on a project.

WHY ARE THERE NO MEDIUM RIFFLERS?

My experience has been that the coarse ones are too coarse and tend to bite, whereas the fine ones are too fine and clog easily—what a pain. For years I experimented with sharpening the fine ones and dulling the coarse ones, but I won't go into that—don't want to make a fool of myself. I found that if I pull rather than push those coarse rifflers at least for the first few passes, they cut but don't bite.

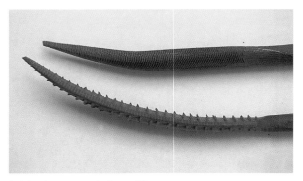
2-34 Coarse and fine rifflers.

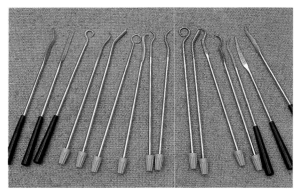
2-35 Diamond rifflers.

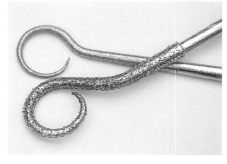
2-36 Coarse and fine diamond rifflers.

Diamond rifflers stay sharp, and they don't clog as much as the steel ones. When working resinous woods, you will still be well advised to have brass brush and solvent handy.

Scrapers

After you have done all you can do with chisel, gouge, and rasps, various scrapers (2–37) can be used to remove tool marks. As most of the surfaces that will need attention will be

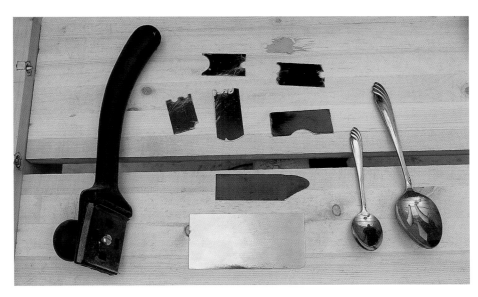

2-37 A collection of various scrapers is very useful.

curved, the standard flat cabinet scraper (2-37, lower center) will find little use. You can, however, round off the corners to get into some places. The scraper formed like a French curve is handy for a lot of work, but it won't do it all. I had one but couldn't find it for the photo. I probably lost or gave it away years ago, and as you read on, you'll see that I don't miss it.

For many flat and convex surfaces, a paint scraper (2-37, left) works well. This tool will remove a lot of material in a surprisingly short time provided that it is kept very sharp. To keep it sharp, take it to a belt sander and hold the edge over the belt at an unsupported area and at a very steep angle (2-38). You might also wish to round off the corners slightly so that they won't dig in and leave lap marks.

Are you laughing at the stainless steel spoons to the left in 2-37? Don't. These make excellent scrapers for concave surfaces. I have several other sizes but didn't want to clutter the photo with them. Rescue a few spoons from your local thrift store, then take them to a sander or grinder and sharpen them perpendicular to the tangent of the surface (2-39).

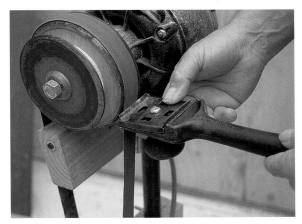

2-38 Sharpening a paint scraper on a belt sander.

2-39 Sharpening a spoon to be used as a scraper.

Essential Woodcarving Hand Tools

Take care when using them that you don't cut yourself on the sharp edge. And never leave them where they might be confused with eating utensils. They're hard on the lips and tongue.

For many projects, you might wish to make your own set of scrapers. This isn't as hard as it might sound. I fashion my special-purpose scrapers from 1¼-inch band-steel (**2-37, upper center**). My lumber dealer receives a lot of material wrapped with this larger steel banding, and I can usually acquire all I want for the polite asking. The steel can be rough-cut with snips, and outside curves can be formed on a grinder or with a file. (This steel is quite hard, so if you use a file, don't expect it to last long.) Inside curves can be easily formed with a tapered stone powered with a drill or die grinder (**2-40**).

Sharpen these scrapers by forming a cutting edge perpendicular to the surface of the steel (**2-41**). Don't try to form a burr on them as you would on a cabinet scraper. Band steel is far too hard.

Remove any burr with a slip stone held against the flat surface, or hold your scraper flat against a belt (**2-42**). It could take a couple of tries at sharpening and burr removal to get a good edge.

Carrying the idea of shop-built scrapers a little further: they can be mounted in a guide for scoring, moldings, and border designs. Simply cut a slot down the center of a thin piece of wood (**2-43** and **2-44**). Cut a notch in the wood to form a guide surface (indicated by the small arrow in **2-45**). Feather the area that will be used as a guide surface. Add a couple of bolts and you just might save the price of a special router bit or shaper cutter that you might only use once (**2-45**).

2-40 **Forming an inside curve on a scraper.**

2-41 **Sharpening the cutting edge of a shop-made scraper.**

2-42 **Removing the burr from the edge of a shop-made scraper.**

38

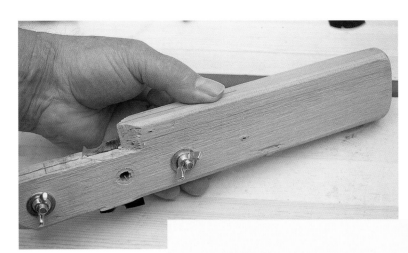

2-43 A guided scraper.

2-44 Assembly of a guided scraper.

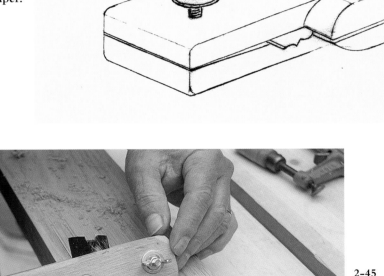

2-45 Guided scrapers can save the cost of special shaper cutters for one-time use.

Essential Woodcarving Hand Tools

SANDING DEVICES

As I mentioned under "Rasps, Rifflers & So Forth," I am no longer a puritanical woodcarver. Wanting to produce the product as well and as efficiently as possible I am in no way averse to using sandpaper where and when it's called for.

In addition to plain sheets of sandpaper I have a number of sanding devices around the studio that you might be interested in. These are various and sundry pieces of wood that I glue sandpaper to with contact cement **(2-46)**.

When I apply the sandpaper initially, I am careful to make a good contact cement bond. When the sandpaper gets dull, I bond another piece over it, using less glue. When this one gets dull, it can be easily peeled off and another applied.

2-46 **Gluing sandpaper to different shapes of wood can ease the sanding process.**

There will be times when forcing the sandpaper into low spots with a stick or dowel is the best way to go **(2-47)**. I have several sizes of dowel domed on one end for the purpose. They may not have been domed initially, but, through use, they get that way.

When all else fails you can hold the sandpaper with your fingertips. After a few hours of

TYPES OF SANDPAPER

The sandpaper I normally use is the type used in machine sanding belts. This type of sandpaper—or perhaps I should call it sanding cloth—incorporates an excellent grit-bonding agent that outlasts any type of "paper." Many companies that manufacture sanding belts sell their end cuts by the pound in assortments. These assortments are very economical and well worth acquiring. The last time I placed a telephone order for one of these assortments, I asked the woman on the other end, "How can you sell it so cheap?"

"Well, you know, our production costs have increased dramatically over the last two years and shipping . . . did you say 'cheap'?"

I love to ask that question; it catches a lot of folks off guard.

sanding, you'll probably find the skin on your fingertips along with your nails becoming increasingly thin. Don't let this happen. Make a trip to the office supply store and buy some of those little rubber "thingies" that office workers put on their fingertips to sort paper **(2-48)**. These come in an assortment of sizes and are more easily replaced than skin and nails.

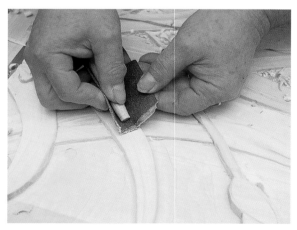

2-47 **Sandpaper can be forced into low spots with a stick or dowel.**

Architectural Carving: Techniques for Power & Hand Tools

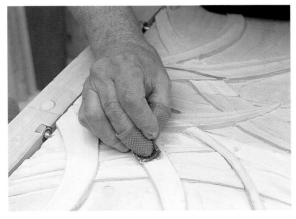

2-48 **Protecting fingertips from sharp sandpaper.**

MEASURING DEVICES

Beyond a simple ruler, an assortment of measuring devices always comes in handy **(2-49)**. As with carving tools, I have more than I really need. I use these for transferring dimensions from drawing to project, especially when working in the round. The ones on the left can be used for inside or outside measurements and do not lock in any particular position. The ones to the right lock either by thumb-

adjusting screw or by a lock bolt on the wing. I use these for fixed and repetitive measurements.

There are two devices that I will particularly call to your attention. The first of these I call a "scaling divider." A measurement taken with the right end is translated to twice that measurement at the left end—great for working with half-scale drawings and working from a centerline **(2-50)**. The pivot bolt has a couple of washers and a spring to give the legs a little bit of drag so that they won't move easily. When working with odd scales, I've been

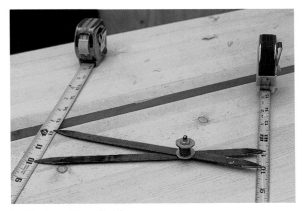

2-50 **A scaling divider.**

2-49 **Measuring devices.**

known to construct a pair of these out of wood to accommodate the odd scale.

The second device is really a fixture for holding a pencil to any size pair of spring dividers (2-51 and 2-52). I have yet to find a good pencil divider or compass if you prefer. I used to tape a pencil to one leg of a divider, but a guy has to look a little professional.

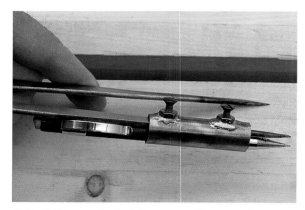

2-52 A fixture for holding a pencil, or mechanical pencil for fine, accurate lines, to a pair of dividers.

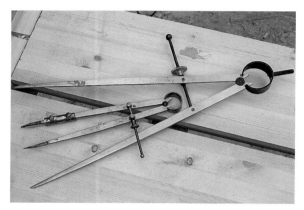

2-51 Spring dividers of any size can be adapted to hold a pencil.

To brew this little fixture in your very own studio, acquire a 2-inch length of ½-inch copper pipe, two No. 8-32 brass nuts, and two 8-32 stainless steel screws about ½-inch long. Drill two holes in the pipe for the screws, thread the nuts on, and drop them into the holes. Solder the nuts securely to the pipe—the solder won't stick to the stainless steel screws. Once the assembly is cool, take it to a vise and squash it to make it slightly oval. If you hate to sharpen pencils for those fine, accurate lines, you can use it with a mechanical pencil (2-52).

HANDY TO HAVE

There are things that you can definitely do without, but if you have them they will be useful (2-53). Among my collection is a drawknife.

I use it rarely, but it was my grandfather's and must have a place of honor on the wall.

The red and green things in 2-53 are spoke-shaves. The green one has a flat base and is used for working straight surfaces. The red one has a curved base and can be used for both straight and curved surfaces.

The item in the center of 2-53 is called a scorp. It's not a tool I would run out and buy, but my father presented me with that one. It is terrifically handy for hollowing out impressions.

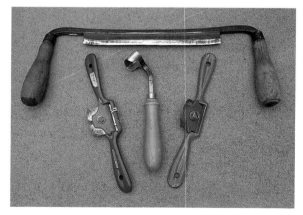

2-53 Other hand tools.

Architectural Carving: Techniques for Power & Hand Tools

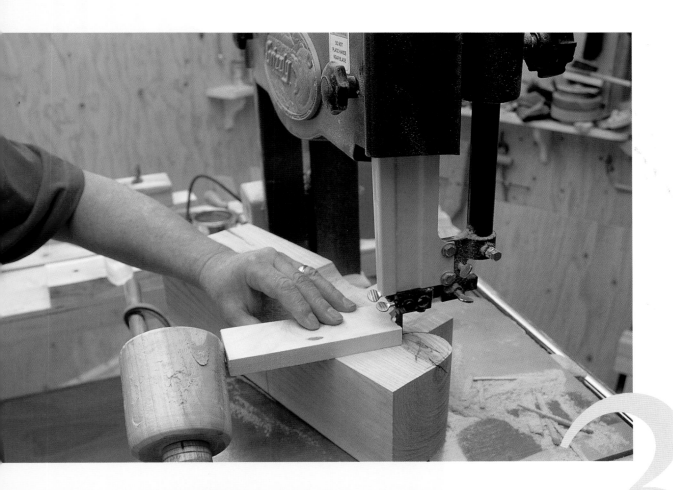

USEFUL POWER TOOLS

It seems to me that today power tools are promoted as the woodworker's panacea. "If you only had this such and such, you could do work just like the professionals, and with the optional accessories, you'll be able to fly, walk on water, and travel in time. And it all comes with a lifetime guarantee." "Yeah, right." Maybe I should say, Yeah, perhaps. Power tools should be used to take the drudgery out of the work.

Hand tools may be essential, but I'd not trade my tenoning machine for all of the scribes, handsaws, and chisels in Connecticut. Nor would I trade my band saw for all of the bow saws ever made. Nevertheless. power tools do not eliminate the skill needed by the operator. In many cases, it takes more skill to operate a hand-fed power tool than it does to use a hand tool for the same job. When I was training my sons in the woodworking craft, I insisted that they become proficient with hand tools before turning on any switch. One reason is obvious: You don't turn an eight-year-old loose on a table saw. All of the boys thank me to this day, for they have come to realize that there is more to woodworking than shoving boards through machines. And, when the power goes off, they can still function.

BAND SAWS

Some years ago a visitor to my shop asked an interesting question: "If I were to take every power saw in the place and leave you only one, which one would it be?" At the time we had three 10-inch table saws, a 16-inch sliding-table dual-arbor table saw, a 24-inch ripsaw, and two band saws.

I thought for a moment—but not a long moment—then pointed to the 36-inch band saw in the corner and said, "I'll keep that one." 'Tis true that a table saw is a very valuable machine in the general woodworking shop, but it won't cut curves. To the architectural carver, a band saw is a must. I suppose that the work of a band saw could be done with a hand, bow saw, but believe me, sawing is not part of my physical fitness program. I prefer pool or billiards; it provides even more stretching and works the same muscles in the right arm.

If you don't yet have a band saw, buy as big a one as you can house and afford. The machine I mentioned above sported a 36-inch throat

and a 24-inch depth of cut. I could cut the side of a bombé chest in one pass. The machine that appears in the photos in this book has an 18-inch throat and a 10-inch depth of cut. It is adequate for most projects. Keep in mind that

BAND-SAW TIPS

Let me present a few things you might not have thought of. I have watched people work who have been using a band saw for years and still not found some of the things that can make the machine whistle rather than sing off key. You might find some of these ideas a little radical, but give them a try.

If you are cutting something large, stand back from it and hold it by its extremity (3-1). Don't hold it in the middle with your nose over the blade. If you are standing back, your peripheral vision will see more of the line you're cutting in advance. This in itself will keep the cut flowing.

Don't push with your arms. Rather, hold your arms and wrists somewhat rigid, pushing with your whole body. Let the body hinge on ankles and hips. You will find that you have far better control. Try this little tip from someone who has cut hundreds of chair legs.

3-1 It's easier to cut smoothly by standing back from the work.

for the carver, depth of cut is usually more important than throat size.

The radius of a curve that a blade will cut is directly related to its width. It would therefore seem that you should use as narrow a blade as possible. Not necessarily so. The strength of a blade is also related to its width. And, guides do not work well with very narrow blades. Narrow blades require gentle love and attention, and to me it's not worth it. I tend to be a little rough.

Hanging near my band saw are a couple of ¼-inch blades, a couple of ½- and ¾-inch blades and a lot of ⅜-inch blades. A ½- or ¾-inch blade I will use if I have a lot of long flowing cuts to make. I also use them for squaring up logs. They tend to wander less in long flowing cuts and have more strength for the logs. I will install a ¼-inch blade if I have a lot of tight cuts to make in thin material.

I don't like to change blades. I dislike changing guides and thrust bearing settling even more. Most of the time you will find a ⅜-inch blade in my saw. It has sufficient strength for logs and with a little ingenuity it can be used for very tight cuts.

When I must make tight cuts with a ⅜-inch blade, I first remove all of the waste that I can (3-2). Then I make a number of relief cuts to the line in the tight places (3-3). With this done, the wider blade will make the radius, popping out the waste between the relief cuts (3-4).

At times when even this trick won't work, I make side-by-side cuts to the line. Then I come back and smooth out any irregularity, using the teeth of the saw as a sort of rasp (3-5).

In these operations you will be freeing a lot of tiny waste pieces. These tend to get caught in the table insert, and you will find yourself continually stopping the machine to clear them. If the insert is not needed to support a tiny project, remove it and let the waste pieces fall through.

3-2 Step one in cutting a tight curve with a wide blade is to remove all waste possible.

3-3 Step two: Make a number of relief cuts.

3-4 Step three: Cutting along the line, remove the waste between relief cuts.

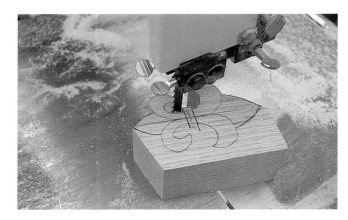

3-5 Saw teeth can be used like a rasp for smoothing cuts.

BAND-SAW BLADES

It would seem that it would be best to do the smoothest work possible in the first stages of a project, such as band-sawing. In as much, the finer teeth of a blade, the better. For material less than 1 inch thick this could be true. For thicker material, it is not true. When you cut, sawdust builds up in the gullets (the spaces between the teeth) of the blade and is discharged as the blade exits the work at the bottom. In a fine-tooth blade the gullets are very small and fill rapidly. If you are cutting a 6-inch piece of maple, you might find that the blade won't cut at all or very slowly. I don't have a blade finer than 6 teeth per inch.

3-6 Stop the machine and use a scrap, tapping with a mallet, to free a bound blade.

There will come a time when you bind a blade in the work. The belt will slip and squeal, and you might tend to panic. Don't. And, don't try to pull the blade out of the work while the motor is running. This could pull the blade out of the guides and, if the saw should start to run again, it could put pressure on the blade, pulling it off of the wheels. Turn off the machine. The squeal will stop, and you will feel a lot better. Make sure the work is not twisting the blade. Then take a scrap and mallet and tap the blade back in the kerf until it's free once more (3-6).

One little band-saw safety note: Don't clear chips from the saw table while the machine is running. But if you must, do it at a time when the blade is buried in the work (3-7).

3-7 Clear chips only when the blade is buried in the work.

ROUTERS

High on the list of useful power tools for the carving studio is a router. Used either freehand or in conjunction with a template, it's a great tool for removing background waste when doing relief work.

If you are working freehand, a handy accessory is a see-through router base (3-8). The transparent base will give you a much better view of the layout lines of the design than you could get looking through the small hole in a nontransparent base.

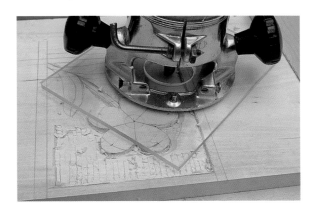

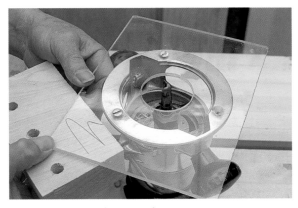

3-8 A see-through router base.

This can be made from ¼-inch, clear acrylic or polycarbonate sheet—polycarbonate being much stronger. Simply use your factory base to mark out the sheet goods (3-9), and drill the holes in the appropriate places. If you use a

3-9 Mark clear plastic sheet using the factory base as a guide.

hole saw to cut the center hole, cut halfway through on one side, then turn the sheet over and cut the rest of the way. This will leave the waste hanging halfway out of the hole saw—much easier to remove than digging it out with a screwdriver.

While on the subject of router bases and a clear view of the bit, I'll give you one more idea. Try using a large hunk of wood and a piece of all-thread, washers, and nuts for U bolts (3-10). This type of base gives as clear a shot at the bit as you will ever have. I like it because of the bulk, which keeps the router from jumping. I do have to wax the bottom of the hunk periodically for smooth operation.

3-10 A clear-vision base contrived from a block of wood and U bolts.

47

For repetitive projects a template makes the work go much faster. There are two methods of working with a template. The first and I suppose the most conventional is to use a bushing on the router base (3-11). The router bit works inside of the bushing and the bushing follows the template. Now, isn't that clever?

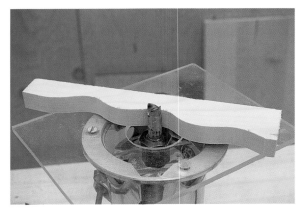

3-12 Router bit with the shank riding the template.

3-11 Template bushing mounted on a router base.

Not really. It's more a pain in the posterior because the template has to be cut short by the distance from the outer edge of the template bushing to the router bit as indicated by the points of the dividers. (I had to borrow a template bushing for the photograph. My beautiful set of template bushings were lost or given away years ago.)

I prefer to cut the template the exact size of the design and let the shank of a short-flute router bit ride the template (3-12). If I don't have a bit of the length I want I make one from ⅜- or ½-inch drill rod (3-13). (I seldom use a bit with a shank smaller than ⅜ inch; I tend to be a bit rough, and ¼-inch shanks yield far too easily.)

If your router didn't come with a ⅜-inch collet—which it probably didn't—you may be able to order one from the manufacturer.

While you are working with clear sheet goods, you might want to make yourself a

3-13 Shop-made bits fabricated from drill rod.

guiding base. This base has the advantage that it will follow a curved surface. It will require no more than a piece of sheet goods, a couple of ¼-inch carriage bolts, nuts, washers, and a stick of wood for the guide itself (3-15). Pointing the guide stick will permit you to follow very tight curves. Slotting the stick will permit adjusting how far the bit cuts into the work.

Another option is to cut a notch out of the guide stick. This will permit the use of only a portion of a bit's profile around a curved surface (3-16).

One other base of interest is a curved base for working concave surfaces. The curve of the

Architectural Carving: Techniques for Power & Hand Tools

MAKING YOUR OWN ROUTER BIT

To make a bit, first split the rod with an abrasive saw blade in a table saw or grinder. The split should be about 1½ times the depth you intend to cut. Then grind back slightly from the leading edge of the split to provide a little relief **(3-14)**—0.003 inch is plenty. As a final step, grind back from the cutting tip at about 30 degrees. This type of bit has the advantage that the shavings clear quickly and don't just keep going around in the cut and overheating the bit. It has the disadvantage that it won't start in the center of the work. There will be a little column of waste standing in the center of the bit preventing it from moving. If you can't start from the edge, make several plunging cuts to remove the column, or start as an airplane would come in for a landing.

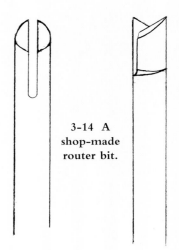

3-14 A shop-made router bit.

The first of these bits I made, I tempered. Of late, I leave them with whatever hardness the drill rod came with. They do get dull more quickly, but I can touch them up with a file, not having to remove the bit from the router. I file the slot toward the cutting edge. That little break in the workday is always welcome, and I always have a keen bit rather than a smoking, carbide cutter.

base should be a bit tighter than the surface of the work being cut. This base can be cut on a band saw but has the disadvantage that the curve of the base must be held parallel to the curve of the work. The ultimate is to turn a dish-shaped base on a lathe **(3-17)**.

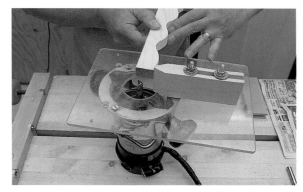

3-15 A router base with a guide.

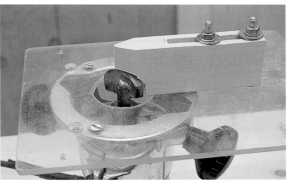

3-16 Cutting a notch in the guide permits use of only a portion of the bit's cutting profile.

3-17 A dish-shaped base for cutting on inside curves.

CAUTION WITH DULL BITS

Here, I will add one little word of caution that you might not be aware of. Dull bits can throw out burning embers. I have forced a bit to finish up that last little portion of work and set more than one shirttail to smoldering. Worse than that, I was once using a pin router to hollow out guitar bodies to accept an electronics package. Forcing the machine to finish up that last little bit of hollowing, a hot ember got sucked into the dust-collecting system that the fire inspector insisted we connect to the pin router.

This ember, accompanied by other shavings, was carried by the gale-force winds of the collector to the shed in the back of the shop. On its way it must have convinced other shavings to glow as brightly as itself, for the tin shed, unbeknownst to any of us in the shop, began to emit a billowing cloud of smoke.

I heard sirens, but this was not unusual, as the shop was located on a busy street, and sirens were common. I didn't even notice that they stopped in front of the shop. I didn't notice, that is, until two firemen burst through the front door, hose in hand.

I felt like a teller in the midst of a bank robbery. I threw my hands in the air and yelled, "Don't shoot!"

The story has a happy and a sad ending. The happy part is that the firemen were able to stop the smoldering by pumping thousands of gallons water into the shed over an hour's time. The sad part is we had to pay the guy that hauls away the shavings an extra fifty bucks to handle them wet.

BURRS & TOOLS TO DRIVE THEM

What are burrs? Essentially, they are round file-type devices whose shank can be mounted in a rotary, drive tool. These can be very handy for fine, detail work, reaching tight places, and working in areas where grain direction poses a challenge. I would not recommend that you depend on burrs for removing any large amount to waste; they are too slow.

I once had an employee whose sole carving equipment consisted of a flexible shaft motor and a handful of burrs. His designs were as impeccable as was his finished product. The only problem was that it took him two days to do a half-day's work, and he would not even consider the use of different types of tool for doing the rough work. He didn't last long with the firm.

Steel Burrs

I have several different types of burr, the first of these being steel **(3-18)**. These are actually

3-18 Steel burrs.

rotary files, and overall the least expensive in my collection. Some are coarse, some are fine, and both come in an assortment of shank sizes and styles. They cut well and cut cleanly while they are sharp. These are probably the most susceptible to damage through overheating. Once the burr is overheated, it can lose its temper and become dull quickly. (See the section "An Unconventional Way to 'Sharpen' a Rasp or File," on pages 69–71, under "Sharpening Steel Rasps, Rifflers, Files & Burrs" in Chapter 4, for some ideas on rejuvenation.)

I find smaller burrs especially handy for detailing such things as hair on both human and animal figures **(3-19)**. And when I'm working on a human face, there is that one spot in the corner of the eye that I just can't seem to cut well with any other tool **(3-20)**.

3-19 **Burrs can be used for fine detail work.**

3-20 **Burrs can be used in tight places with impossible grain changes.**

OVERHEATED BURRS

All burrs can be damaged through overheating. This usually occurs when the burr is dull to start with, or when you force it, asking it to take away more material than it was designed to remove.

Always begin with light, delicate cuts, increasing pressure slowly. The burr will tell you when you are approaching its limit. Once a burr has been overheated, it loses its effectiveness, essentially becoming worthless. Be careful with your expensive burrs.

Carbide Burrs

More expensive than steel burrs, carbide burrs are well worth the cost **(3-21,** upper center**)**. They remain sharp and cut cleanly much longer. Actually, I could afford to pay ten times the price of a steel burr and come out financially ahead, but the price of carbide burrs is not that high. Carbide burrs are probably the least susceptible to damage through overheating. Excess heat can cause the more delicate areas of the carbide to fracture, actually sharpening the burr, although fracturing does distort the shape. As you can see I have a rather scant assortment of carbide burrs. All are straight cutters, but I find

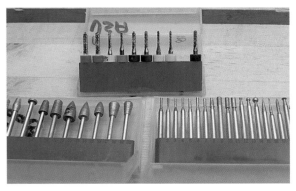

3-21 **Diamond burrs (two sets at bottom) and carbide burrs (at top).**

51

these especially handy for making parting cuts along the grain **(3-22)**, an area that often defies parting cleanly.

3-22 **Straight burrs facilitate parting cuts with the grain.**

Diamond Burrs

These are steel tools of various shapes and sizes coated with diamond particles, much the same as the diamond rifflers I described above **(3-21,** lower**)**. Diamond burrs are almost like sanding devices, but they will remove substantial material cleanly and quickly, as they turn so fast. They remain sharp indefinitely, although they can be damaged by heat. Heat doesn't damage the diamond but attacks the agent that bonds the diamond to the steel, and the diamonds disappear. If this happens to any of my long, straight burrs, I simply clip off the damaged tip with an old pair of wire cutters and continue using the burr.

Drivers

I have an electrically powered driver that my kids presented me one year for Christmas **(3-23,** right**)**. Though not terrifically powerful, it is a great little tool. Its greatness lies in its variable speeds, sometimes required in detailing. I find it especially handy for tool maintenance. If you were to walk into my studio right

now, you would probably find a diamond-impregnated rubber wheel mounted in it for polishing the channel of gouges.

When I need more power than the electrically powered tool can deliver, I use a pneumatic mini die grinder **(3-23,** center**)**. For years I drooled over such devices in catalogues but never thought I could justify the cost. Besides, I had the electrically powered device. I bought the one in the photo because . . . well, I bought it because it was on sale. I freely admit it. I'm not proud. My lady had a good laugh. Laughs aside, after using the tool for a while, I could have justified the cost much sooner.

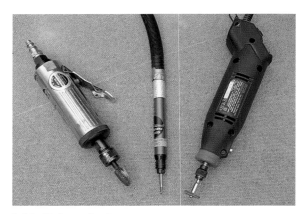

3-23 **Drivers for burrs.**

It does have one serious drawback. Its sound reminds me of my dentist with his broad, friendly smile and his gleaming white teeth. It also reminds me of the torture this wonderful man inflicts on me with each visit. On my last visit, he gave me a handful of old dental burrs to use with my new machine. That eased the pain.

For larger burrs, I prefer a pneumatic die grinder. These little devices are relatively inexpensive and have plenty of power, but they do require at least a three-horsepower compressor to keep them supplied with power.

There are also flexible shafts, which can be attached to an electric motor, that have plenty of power although they don't run very fast. I had one. I don't now. The first time it got away from me and flipped up, hitting me in the mouth, I invested in a die grinder.

ELECTRICALLY POWERED CHISELS

How lazy can we get that we must substitute electric power for muscle and mallet? In the same box with the rotary tool my kids gave me resided an electrically powered chisel and three or four carving tools to fit it. I don't know what became of the tools; I was not overly impressed with them. After fashioning some tools of my own I found this little tool great for small detailed work (3-24). It comes in very handy for veining leaves where it's often hard to get a flowing cut through grain changes. Thumbing through a newer catalogue, I noticed an electrically powered chisel considerably larger than mine. I'm not really tempted to buy one; read on and you'll see why.

3-24 **An electric chisel with shop-made cutters.**

PNEUMATICALLY POWERED CHISELS

If you're going to substitute mallet and muscle with something, substitute it with something that has real power. Stone carvers use an inline pneumatic device to power their tools. It works very much the same as the electrical one I described above. You put a carving tool in the end of the device and as you push, the device begins to hammer. The harder you push, the harder it hammers.

Now this may sound rather sissy, but I'll bet that if Michelangelo had one of these tools, he would have used it. Think of the additional works he could have produced. Of course, he didn't have such a tool, and that's because da Vinci hadn't yet designed an air compressor.

I had the opportunity to use one of these tools in another's shop. I think that if I had had a chance to play with it for a couple of days, I could have gotten used to it. And, I would now be recommending it highly. I didn't have the time to play with the tool, nor did I have the cash to run out and buy one of my own— they are a bit expensive.

Rather, I took a little different approach and bought a pistol-type air hammer at the auto parts store. This air hammer was far more economical—I've seen small ones on sale for about what it costs to go to the movies.

There are two types of pistol air hammer readily available (3-25). One is small, lightweight, and delivers a fantastic number of blows per minute. It is the least powerful and least costly. I use the one I have for cleanup cuts in softer woods.

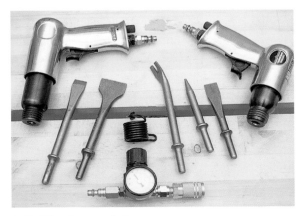

3-25 **Pistol-type air hammers.**

The other is more costly, far more powerful, but delivers fewer blows per minute. This little jewel is great for rough work and removes a tremendous amount of wood in a short time.

Both tools are designed to work off of a 90-psi (pounds per square inch) air-supply line. In most cases I find that 90 psi is a bit more power than I need, so I have an inline regulator on my supply line and vary the pressure between 40 and 60 psi.

None of the readily available accessory tools for these devices are designed for carving wood. Some of the tools are quite stubby and almost worthless. Other tools are about 4½ inches long and have potential. The only tool that came with my hammers that I use in its pristine state is the sheet-metal cutter.

If it is a simple chisel you desire these are easy to find and can be resharpened to carve wood. A 20-degree cutting angle works best for me. Remember that you are going to be delivering a tremendous amount to pressure the cutting edge and a more blunt tool is in order—especially in hard-textured woods.

If you need a gouge, you're going to have to make your own by modifying a readily available tool. For a shallow gouge, simply hollow the face of a thick chisel, then sharpen it to cut wood (3–26). For a tighter sweep, use a thicker chisel and a smaller stone to do the hollowing (3–27).

For a tight sweep in a wider tool, you'll have to do a little simple blacksmithing. Heat a wide chisel with a MAPP gas torch to a bright red glow (the steel should glow brighter than that in the following photos). Place it across the inside radius of some heavy metal object and give it a stout blow with the round end of a ball-peen hammer (3–28); this will start the curve. If you want a tighter sweep, reheat the tool and strike it on both edges (3–29). If you do have an anvil, the sweep can be trued up on the horn.

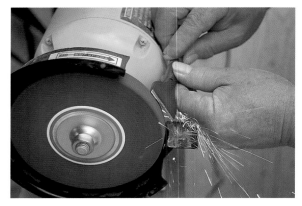

3-26 Hollowing a straight chisel to form a shallow gouge.

3-27 Hollowing with a smaller wheel to form a tighter sweep.

After all this heating and forming the tool will have to be retempered.

When I first started carving with an air chisel, I found that little spring "thingie" that came with the hammers to be worthless. It did keep the chisel from flying from the hammer, but it didn't keep the chisel from rotating. The spring was quickly retired to my junk drawer. I then discovered that holding the chisel with my fingers didn't give me much more control, and it was tiring. Enter handles.

For tools with a flat shank, I mortised the shank into two blocks of wood and glued them together with a generous amount of glue (3–30). For tools with a round shank, I drilled a hole to fit the shank in a block of wood—

Architectural Carving: Techniques for Power & Hand Tools

3-28 Forming a gouge with simple blacksmithing.

3-29 Tightening the sweep.

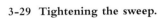

RETEMPERING THE TOOL

First heat the end of the tool once more and keep it red hot for about a minute. Back the tool out of the flame and let the red glow slowly disappear—the process should take about two minutes. Then let the tool cool to room temperature naturally. This process, called annealing, relieves any stresses in the steel caused by the forming.

After the tool has reached room temperature, once again heat the end to a bright red glow. Keep it at that temperature for about one minute, then quench it in a container of room-temperature water. Next polish the end with 220-grit sandpaper and place it in your kitchen range oven set at 450 degrees for about a half hour. The polished area should have turned a dark straw color. This is a little soft for a handheld carving tool but will prevent the power tool from nicking. Let the tool cool and you're ready to sharpen.

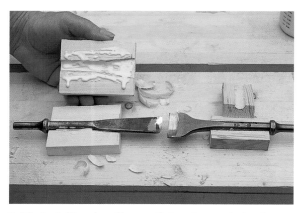

3-30 Installing handles on flat and round-shank tools.

sometimes a large dowel. After splitting the block with a chisel, I glued it over the shank. You'll note the pockmarks made with a grinder in the round shank. These fill with glue and prevent the tool rotating in the handle.

After a little whittling to give the blocks some semblance of comfort, the tools are ready to use (3-31). But don't use them just yet. First, don a good pair of safety glasses or face shield. Normally I don't wear glasses when carving, but I make an exception when using the air chisel. With all of that power, chips can leave the work at considerable velocity, and getting hit in the face is, at the least, uncomfortable.

All in all I'm quite satisfied with the performance of the pistol-type driver over the

3-31 Handles whittled for comfort.

NOTES ON PNEUMATIC TOOLS

Read all instructions that come with your pneumatic tool carefully. Take special note of the lubrication specifications. If these tools are not kept lubricated, they will freeze up. You will be instructed to use a couple of drops of oil—I use SAE 30—in the air hose or an inline oiler. I have never had an inline oiler, but I do put oil in the air inlet of the tool about once every half hour of heavy use. It's easy to tell if you're using too much oil; it will blow out on the work.

Invest in a line regulator for your pneumatic tools and don't use more pressure than necessary. If the tool will operate satisfactorily at 40 psi don't run it at 90 psi. If your compressor is running continually, that tiny die grinder is eating up the full horsepower of your compressor motor—in my case 3 horsepower. That's a lot of energy to be wasting on such a small tool.

inline device. I think the thing that pleases me most is that the position of the hands is the same as if using a mallet.

ANGLE GRINDERS

An angle grinder is another tool that's handy to have around (3-32). I have two such tools, a lightweight one and one that is much heavier and more powerful. I use both mostly for sanding and sculpting. I say sculpting because fitted with 36-grit sandpaper they can remove a lot of material in a short time. Fitted with a finer paper they are, of course, suitable for smoothing gentle convex surfaces. They can also be fitted with a random-orbit device for finish work on a large scale (3-32, lower right).

Another interesting device that will fit on the spindle is a piece of saw chain held between two metal disks (3-32, lower left).

Architectural Carving: Techniques for Power & Hand Tools

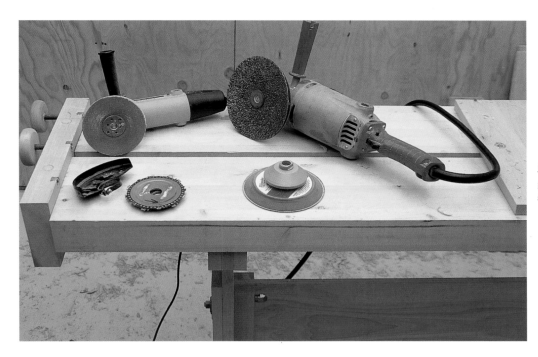

3-32 Angle grinders and accessories.

This is a sculpting device, and it will remove a substantial amount of material quickly. It won't, however, remove material nearly as quickly as an air chisel. As a result, I use my chain attachment rarely. It scares me. If you do use one of these little beauties, I strongly recommend safety glasses and installing the guard pictured to the attachment's left. One slip with that whirling chain could leave some interesting scars, on both you and whatever else it might hit.

Thumbing through catalogues, I've seen other attachments consisting of barbs and carbide teeth. I'm sorry that I can't advise you on these, as I don't have any. With all of the other tools at my disposal, I could never see a need for them.

POWER SANDERS

Beyond the disk grinders, I do have some other power-sanding devices (3-33). The one to the right is a small random orbit sander that takes ¼-sheet of regular sandpaper—very economical. It's great for finishing large convex surfaces.

The two triangular sanders to the left are great for detail and tight places. They both use costly hook-and-loop sandpaper, and I've found the component of the hook-and-loop

57

3-33 Power-sanding tools.

attached to the machine wears out quickly through hard use. At that point, I use contact cement to hold a cheaper paper. The sander to the extreme left in **3-33** has one good point. The tips of the triangle—the area that gets the most use—can be replaced individually.

Missing in the photo is a flap sander or brush sander. This is a device with flaps of sandpaper that is driven by a drill or die grinder. Some have scored sandpaper that is supported by stiff brushes. I had one—don't anymore. I found that these devices tend to knock the corners off of sharp detail, and it's this detail that the carver strives for.

PERSONAL PHILOSOPHY ON CARVING MACHINES

Yes, there are machines that will do the whole job of carving. Some of the new computer-controlled machines work from a program. More common are machines that trace a pattern with a stylus that positions cutter spindles on blank pieces of the work. I have never owned a "real" carving machine, but I've built several.

The most dramatic of these home-brews was specifically designed to rough-cut propellers for ultra-light aircraft. It sported four cutter spindles, each belt-driven by a three-phase, 3-horse power motor. It was so noisy that the operator had to place foam hearing protectors in his ear canal and then wear earmuff-type hearing protectors. Despite the noise, chips flew from the 1½-inch maple blanks, and the machine turned out four rough props every fifteen minutes, adding substantially to the coffers of the company.

Unfortunately too many of the ultralight enthusiasts went to "their reward" prematurely and the propeller business sort of petered out. We modified the machine to carve duck decoys, but they went out of fashion in a short time. As the face of the business changed we found little use for the machine and it wound up being disassembled and its various parts put to better use, particularly the motors.

Any carving machine worth buying is expensive. If you are contemplating such a purchase, I'll pass on one little piece of advice: purchase a machine that will produce at least four items at once. A good carver can outwork a two-head machine in most cases.

SHARPENING WOODCARVING TOOLS

The subject of sharpening is one, Gentle Reader, that I would prefer to avoid. There has been so much written with authority, drama, and enthusiasm on the subject that I am bound to step on someone's toes. At any rate, I will attack the subject because of its extreme importance. To avoid repetition, I'm going to try to touch on points that I think have had far too little mention.

I once asked an older, fellow woodworker, "What is the single most important thing that a woodworker must learn?"

After considerable deliberation, he replied, "Well, he's gotta learn to sharpen his tools." I suppose that in these days of carbide-faced cutting edges that no longer applies to general woodworking, but no one will ever be able to successfully carve wood until they learn to sharpen their tools. Thus I have devoted this entire chapter to the subject.

During woodcarver's club meetings I have listened to presentations on sharpening. One fellow swore by the use of wet-or-dry sandpaper—never clogs, and when it gets dull, throw it away. Another was partial to rubbing tools over anodized aluminum. A third discovered that the unglazed underside of a dinner plate worked well, while a third had the ultimate solution: she had purchased a "sharpening station"—one of those machines that have water dripping on a horizontal wheel. It was great and only cost several hundred dollars. All of these methods are viable but, to my way of thinking, not necessarily the most cost effective nor the most efficient.

FACTORS THAT AFFECT TOOL SHARPNESS

If you have a number of carving tools, you probably have a couple of favorites. Even if they don't exactly match the operation, you pick them up first. They just seem to cut better than any of the others. Why? There are a number of factors that influence just how sharp a tool can get, how long it will stay sharp, and how well it will cut.

Tool Hardness

If you have ever had the opportunity to study Grandpa's straight razor, you probably found it extremely sharp, and Grandpa seemed to keep it that way by merely passing it over a strip of leather. That razor was made of good-quality steel but it was left almost "file hard" (as hard as possible) in its manufacture. Steel of that nature is relatively easy to form a keen edge and holds that keen edge very well. If you dropped Grandpa's razor on the floor and it landed on its edge, you may have noticed a nick in the edge, or perhaps the razor broke in two—hope you were quick enough on your feet to avoid Grandpa's wrath. Steel of that nature is also very brittle, not much stronger than glass.

On the other hand, if the steel is left as soft as it can be, it is almost impossible to form a keen cutting edge thereon. In the case of a carving tool under hard use, the edge would actually fold over.

Tool manufacturers attempt to strike a happy medium, leaving the tool hard enough to take and hold a keen edge while soft enough to prevent nicks and breakage. In my opinion some leave the tools too soft, but to me the reason is obvious. Some inexperienced folks not only cut with the tool but they also tend to pry with it. Some also like to use these tools to remove the lids of paint and patch cans—an effort that would subject one to immediate dismissal from my studio. Surely no manufacturer wants to explain broken or nicked tools, and they can attribute the inability of the tool to form and hold a keen edge to the talents of the person doing the sharpening.

There are some very sophisticated instruments used to test hardness, but there is a simple test that you can perform. Pass a well-used file firmly over the heel of the bevel of the tool in question (4-1). The file should slip over the tool without cutting. If it does cut significantly, you have a soft tool. You'll find that it is hard to form a razor-sharp cutting edge on that tool and when you do get an acceptable edge formed, it won't last long.

My tools vary in hardness. The tools I use for roughing in oak or maple are tempered to

4-1 **Testing for hardness with a file.**

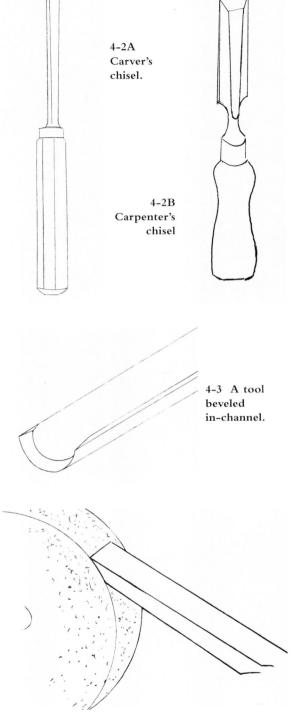

4-2A
Carver's
chisel.

4-2B
Carpenter's
chisel

4-3 A tool
beveled
in-channel.

4-4 **As a tool comes from the grinder, it will have a concave bevel.**

"dark straw" (the color of the steel as it is heated in the tempering process), a little softer than an off-the-shelf carving tool. Others are left at light straw or even harder. These I use only on soft-textured woods and seldom with a mallet. I will admit that I have experienced some nicked edges and even broken tools, but while they worked, they worked well. As such, I would not recommend retempering any of your tools, at least until you get out of the stage of using them as a crowbar. We'll discuss that more in Section II, "Layout, Carving & Finishing Techniques."

BEVELS & CUTTING ANGLES

Carving tools are ground or "beveled" back from the cutting edge toward the body of the tool. Unlike carpenter's chisels, carver's chisels are beveled from the center of the body toward each face (**4-2A** and **4-2B**). Skews are beveled likewise. V tools and most gouges are beveled toward the outside of the tool, but they may be beveled toward the channel for specialty cutting (**4-3**). A gouge thus formed is very useful for rounding off edges and forming beads, while an in-channel V tool cuts straight lines . . . only.

The bevel of the tool as it comes from the grinder is usually concave, conforming to the diameter of the grinding wheel (**4-4**). This is usually flattened out in the honing process.

61

Tools that are left concave or "hollow ground" are quite difficult to control. Tools with a flat bevel are most useful for making straight or flat cuts **(4-5)**. But, with the exception of chip carving, you will find yourself making few straight cuts. If the tool's bevel is slightly rounded **(4-6)**, the tool is very easy to control, and we'll see how to perform this rounding a little later.

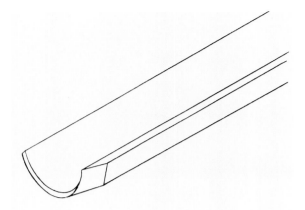

4-7 A tool beveled slightly in-channel for extra strength.

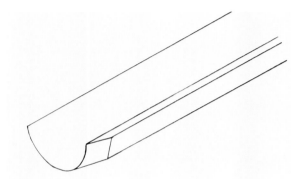

4-5 A tool with a straight, or flat, bevel.

Just what should the angle of this bevel be? Here there is controversy, but let me say that one angle does not fit all. Simple physics dictates that the more acute the angle the easier it will be to push or drive through the wood **(4-8)**. The more acute angle also means a more fragile cutting edge. While I wish that all of my carving tools could have the 3-degree bevel of Grandpa's straight razor, I fear that such a cutting edge would not last long. For tools that I use in soft-textured woods—basswood, pine, alder, etc.—I leave a bevel of 10 to 12 degrees

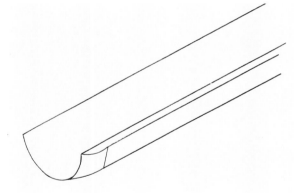

4-6 A tool with a curved bevel.

In addition to the primary bevel, the tool might be beveled slightly on the opposite side **(4-7)**. This has the advantage of providing a stronger cutting edge while also permitting a low angle of attack. In the case of gouges, it also changes the sweep slightly. I don't believe that I have any tools with a secondary bevel that was formed intentionally.

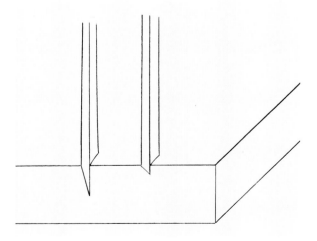

4-8 An acute edge will penetrate deeper than a blunt edge with the same effort.

Architectural Carving: Techniques for Power & Hand Tools

62

average. (I say average because my tools have a slightly rounded bevel.) I will also use these tools for hand cleanup on harder woods—oak, hickory, maple, etc. For tools that I use with a mallet on those harder woods, I leave the bevel at from 15 to 20 degrees.

It's not always easy to judge the bevel of a tool by sight alone. I have a little gauge that I cut with a pair of tin snips from a piece of galvanized steel (4-9). I even painted it black so that I can see it better. The finest cut is about 10 degrees, used for knives. The heaviest cut is 25 degrees, used for heavy-duty tools.

4-9 A gauge for determining the bevel of tools.

I'm inclined to recommend that beginners leave their tools at more obtuse angles than those mentioned above. You see, beginners are inclined to use their tools as splitting wedges or pry bars rather than cutting instruments. Though I'm tempted to recommend that more obtuse angle, I won't. The sharper angles are far easier to use and, after the beginner has to hone out nicks or reform a broken edge a few times, the splitting and prying will stop.

Why You Do What You Do

The object of the game is to form the cutting edge to the smoothest and finest possible, one molecule thick at the cutting edge, if you will.

While one molecule thick might be impossible that is the object. To accomplish this, abrasives are used in increasing fineness of grit, and there are oh so many abrasives and ways to use them.

Both sides of the tool at the cutting edge should be polished to a mirror surface. I emphasize "both," because too often I've seen tools, especially gouges, polished on the beveled side while the channel still has scratches from factory grinding that are completely intact. Note in 4-10 that the gouge to the left has its channel polished to a mirror surface (that line a little further up the shank is rust preventative). The two gouges to the right in 4-10 have significant grinder scratches. If you were to look at the edge of these tools under a microscope, they would

4-10 Scratches in the channels of gouges.

look like a saw. Let's consider just one scratch in 4-11. I suppose that saw teeth on a cutting edge are not all bad, if you use the right technique. I once visited a beginning carver and found him at work using his tools in a rather curious way. Rather than just pushing a gouge forward, he pushed and twisted the tool at the same time. I asked to see the gouge. The edge bore a couple of nicks and some deep scratches left from his coarse stone. Yes, the edge looked like a saw, but he was using it like a saw.

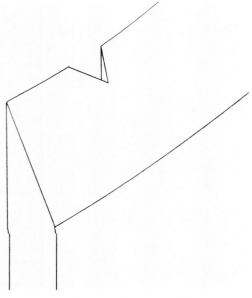

4-11 A single scratch under high magnification. The sides are quite blunt.

TESTING FOR SHARPNESS

You have probably seen a person test an edge for sharpness by passing their thumb across a cutting edge. I guess that this is a good preliminary indicator. Just be sure you move your thumb perpendicular to the edge. This is also a good way to check burrs and carbide tools, which aren't really sharp. The burr's cutting edges and the carbide should tend to stick in the whirls of the fingertip.

I've also seen people test a tool by seeing how easily it will nick their thumbnail. I don't recommend this practice. I once presented a friend with a couple of carving tools, and, of course, I sharpened the gifts before presentation. He tested one on his thumbnail and almost cut through.

SOME THOUGHTS ON THE CUTTING EDGE

At this point let me give you something to think about. All of the books that I have read and all of the lecturers I have listened to recommend polishing both sides of the cutting edge to a mirror brightness as I described above. But! I have a skew that I use very often for rounding operations, especially for rounding end grain. I use the tool with a slicing action. When I made that skew I was in a hurry and I didn't hone the edge carefully or with the finest abrasive. I merely took it to my power strop and polished until it looked good to the naked eye. The skew worked very well. Later in the day when I looked at the edge under magnification, I could see that the edge was full of scratches running perpendicular to the cutting edge. The strop had rounded and somewhat smoothed the scratches but they were still there, making the edge look somewhat serrated under high magnification.

I began to think about that serrated knife in my kitchen, the one I'm partial to for slicing meat. I thought of how it seems to cut so much better than the French chef's knife that's so sharp I could shave with it. (I say that I could shave with it, but you've probably noticed in some of the photos that I don't shave—haven't for thirty years). Since this episode I have not concerned myself with fine scratches provided the edge is polished to the very bottom of the serration that they cause (**4-12**).

I'm not here proposing new technology, just giving you something to think about.

4-12 A scratch that has been polished through vigorous stropping.

64

ONE VERY IMPORTANT NOTE

Before you begin any sharpening operation, have on hand some means of magnification. An 8X or 10X loupe available at photo supply stores works very well. An old camera lens will do, or a large magnifying glass will suffice. Even if you have perfect vision you will be utterly surprised at the things you will see under magnification. So many times, in the past, I would carry a tool through the complete sharpening operation only to find that it didn't cut well. Now I examine the tool at each stage under magnification to make sure that stage is complete before proceeding to the next. Try it—you'll like it.

A better test is to take the tool to a piece of very soft-textured wood and make a cut across the grain. The tool should cut cleanly with absolutely no tearing. As they say, "The proof of the puddin' is in the eatin'."

If you don't have any soft-textured wood on hand, try cutting a stack of newspaper (4–13). This works well in dry climates. If you live in a damp climate and manage to cut soggy newspaper, please send me your sharpening technique.

4-13 Testing for sharpness with newspaper.

TOOL SHAPE

Here I had better mention tool shape. As a general rule of thumb, the tool's cutting edge should be straight and perpendicular to the axis of the shank. The corners should be square, sharp, and well-defined (4–14). Rounded corners can be troublesome when making stop cuts in a setting-in operation, as they will leave a small area uncut. This area will be chipped out, leaving a rather untidy looking project.

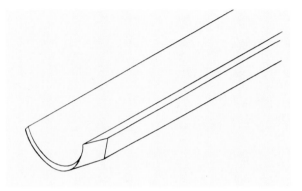

4-14 A well-shaped tool—note the square corners.

There are times when rounded corners are in order. Note in 4–15 the bullet designs. The stop cut for the one on the left was made with a gouge with rounded corners—a bull-nose gouge. The stop cut on the right was made with a gouge with nice square corners. Note the overcut of the square gouge. Gouges used for stop cuts should fit the cut required.

4-15 Sometimes tools should have rounded corners.

65

Sharpening Woodcarving Tools

Corners can be chipped very easily. They can also be rounded off through plain wear and careless stropping. As you study the photos in this book, you may see me using tools with slightly rounded corners. You might also see tools whose cutting edge is slightly askew. I don't run to the grinder to reshape a tool just because it is slightly misshapen. If the tool is performing well in the task at hand, I use it. Only when a tool must have square corners do I reshape it.

STONES & OTHER SHARPENING DEVICES

I have several good-quality sharpening stones **(4-16)**. The large, flat stone toward the top of **4-16** is an "India" stone. It is coarse on one side and fine on the other, great for general sharpening in the first stages. Were that stone flat, it would be fine for sharpening chisels, skews, and plane irons, but that one is worn far from flat. It will remain in my collection with no attempt to flatten it, because it belonged to my grandfather and he spent a lot years wearing the stone unevenly.

Resting on top of the India stone is a small stone whose flat surface is good for chisels and skews. I have rounded one edge so that I can use it in the channel of gouges. The package said it was a "Hard Arkansas" stone, but I rather doubt the label. It is rather soft compared to the little piece of stone in the center of the photo that I know to be hard Arkansas, which is almost translucent.

The conical stone to the right is another India stone, great for the channel of gouges. As it is quite coarse, I use it for the initial work and follow up with one of the ceramic stones from the leather pouch at the bottom of the photo. The ceramic stones are very fine but cut quickly.

The device to the right in **4-16** is a piece of diamond-coated steel with a red plastic

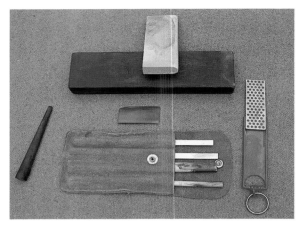

4-16 **Sharpening stones.**

handle. It works for chisels and skews, but trying to sharpen the bevel of a small-sweep gouge can be disastrous. The cutting edge falls into the holes in the steel and can be destroyed. It can be used to sharpen carbide-faced router bits, but as I have very few of these, so it doesn't get much work doing this. I have modified this device to polish the channel of V tools and I'll tell you about it a little further on.

I resort to stones when I can find no other means of doing the job. And as such, I'm not going to go into any extensive explanation of technique. Mine is probably flawed. I will refer you to the "Power Strop" of Chapter 19, in Part IV, "Useful Tools & Equipment You Can Build." I feel that the time of competent carvers is far too valuable to spend rubbing their tools over a rock to get them sharp, although such a practice can be a welcome diversion in the day's toil. Slowly, deliberately, and lovingly rubbing your favorite tool over a stone that has served for many years can be quite soothing.

Lubricants

Most stones require some form of lubricant. The word "lubricant" here is somewhat misleading. To me the word conjures a vision of a substance that prevents wear. In the case of a sharpening stone, that's the last thing you want it to do; rather, you want it to wear as much and as quickly as possible.

On a sharpening stone the lubricant holds the particles of removed metal in suspension so that they may be wiped away rather than falling in between the grit of the stone and clogging it. Oil is recommended for some stones, water for others. I've found that kerosene works well. I've also found that oil and kerosene are messy and flammable. I use neither.

Cup your hand over this paragraph so that no uninterested eyes may view it. There is another lubricant of merit. Given that it is your tool, your stone, and your studio—and there is no one around—consider saliva.

4-17 Using a strop.

4-18 Using a strop for the channel.

Cleaning Stones

Stones will become dirty and clogged even if a good lubricant is used. To clean them merely scrub them in soapy water with a stiff brush—a fine-wire brush works best.

Strop

The last stage in any sharpening operation is stropping or polishing the cutting edge. This is usually done on the hair side (smooth side) of a piece of leather impregnated with some sort of polishing compound—jeweler's rouge, emery, Tripoli, etc. (See Chapter 19, "Power Strop" in Part IV, "Useful Tools & Equipment You Can Build." for more information on compounds.) Leather glued to a board using contact cement works very well. Rounding one edge of the board and wrapping the leather around permits stropping the channel of gouges.

To use the strop, firmly pull the tool across the leather away from the cutting edge **(4-17)**. Plenty of pressure makes the job go more quickly. Twist the gouges as you pull and don't forget the channel side **(4-18)**.

SHARPENING A NEW V TOOL

Though I've mentioned little on the techniques of hand sharpening, I am going to mention the V tool and some techniques for making it work well. A new V tool will have a rather obtuse angle at its base **(4-19, bottom)**. The first step, before you use the tool, is to grind that angle more acutely **(4-19, top)**.

4-19
A new and
a prepared
V tool.

Sharpening Woodcarving Tools

67

If you don't grind the base of the V, your V tool will have a very high angle of attack compared to one that has been ground (4-20).

Next, you will note that there is a radius at the base of the new V tool rather than a sharp V. Here is where I use that diamond-coated sharpening device mentioned under "Stones." After grinding the device to fit the channel of the V tool, I work that radius into a sharp V (4-21) or at least one with a much shorter radius. It takes time and a little "elbow grease," but it can be done.

4-20 Angle of attack of a new and a prepared V tool.

4-21 Sharpening the channel of a V tool using a modified diamond "stone."

SHARPENING STEEL RASPS, RIFFLERS, FILES & BURRS

Why would anyone want to attempt to sharpen any of these tools? They are inexpensive and easily replaced. Perhaps I should apologize for my attitude, but my grandmother always said, "Waste not, want not." It is oh so hard for me to discard anything that may still be useful. I can't do it; I can't even bear the thought. I make scrapers and measuring tools, as I've explained, from band steel cut from lumber packs and discarded by deliverymen. Old files often become shaper and router cutters. Rifflers often turn into specialty carving tools. Burrs sometimes become small punches or countersinks. Perhaps I just like to tinker.

But—and this is a big but—I have found that some new, fine rifflers and especially steel burrs right off the shelf are too dull to be useful. Some fine rifflers do a better job of burnishing than cutting. One in five burrs will do little more than burn its way through hard maple. Note the new burr to the right in 4-22.

4-22 Sharp and dull burrs.

Compare it to the one on the left that was recently sharpened. Look again in 4-23 after it has had a soothing bath. So many times the first thing I do with these items is sharpen them. If you think I put words on paper in jest, dig out your loupe and look carefully at your new tool.

Architectural Carving: Techniques for Power & Hand Tools

4-23 A dull burr after sharpening.

An Unconventional Way to "Sharpen" a Rasp or File

Many years ago I found that corrosion could be good for dull rasps and files. I was working on a project outdoors when a horseshoe rasp, unbeknownst to me, fell into the shavings beneath my feet. It began to rain and I moved the project indoors but made no attempt to clean up the shavings until two weeks of gentle rains later. When I did clean up the shavings, I found the rasp, entangled in shavings and rendered almost shapeless with rust. I could have cried but didn't. That rasp, dulled by years of good service, had reached the end of its days and waited only for replacement.

Tool lover that I am, I carried the "corpse" inside and ran a wire brush over it to clean and prepare it for burial. Before the funeral I tried it on a piece of wood just once for old times' sake. Lo and behold, it worked better than when new. Well, that's not quite true. The areas that were clogged with pitch and untouched by the water were still dull, but the real rusty areas were very sharp.

That day I began to experiment. I won't bore you with the details, but I will give you the final results. I will tell you what has worked for me, but I can't recommend that you do this. And if you do, do so at your own risk, taking all safety precautions pointed out seriously.

NOTE: THE FOLLOWING IS A RUBBER GLOVE AND SAFETY GLASSES OPERATION.

As a corrosive agent I settled on toilet bowel cleaner—the kind that has hydrochloric acid. It's the acid that does the work, but the other ingredients work as a wetting agent, carrying the acid into the tight recesses of the tool being sharpened. They will also work to clean any dirt and oil that might remain on the item being sharpened.

For large rasps, and for lack of a better container, I prepare a tray by lining a box with plastic film (4-24). To keep the rasp off the bottom of the tray and separated from any others that I might put in, I use rubber bands. After thoroughly cleaning the rasp with lacquer thinner and a wire brush, I place it in the tray and cover it with at least ¼-inch of toilet

4-24 A tray prepared with plastic film.

bowl cleaner, then go about my business. Each time I pass the tray I agitate it gently. In a couple of hours, I check the progress by rinsing off the rasp and trying it on a piece of wood. If it's not as sharp as I think it should be, it's back to the tray for another couple of hours.

For rifflers I can use a smaller plastic container that will hold enough solution to cover the working end and support the shank (4-25). I have a good supply of such containers. My lady comes home with armloads of these after attending a party. If the container you're using could be construed as a food container, I highly recommend that you draw a skull and crossbones on it so that it may never again be used for food.

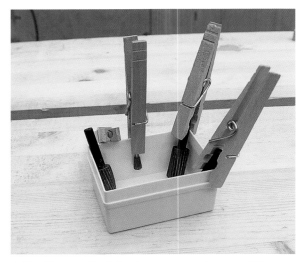

4-26 One method for keeping shanks out of the sharpening bath.

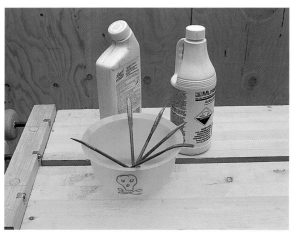

4-25 A steep-sided bowl can be used for rifflers.

For sharpening burrs, I have to contrive a system for keeping the shanks out of the solution (4-26). After a little "sharpening," the shanks will be too small to fit the chuck.

I wish that I could give some firm figures on time. The process is more a time–temperature process. If it's 80 degrees, a rasp can be restored in four to eight hours. If it's 50 degrees it could take 24 to 48 hours. (Don't think about heating the solution. That could be dangerous.) Also, provide for good ventila-

tion in the shop, or better, work outdoors. There are some interesting fumes given off in the operation. And never leave the solution near any of your cutting tools. In a short time you will find them coated with a copper-colored film—that looks sort of like rust, but it's probably some chlorine compound of iron. In addition to the coating you'll find that the razor-sharp cutting edge is gone and the tools will have to be sharpened.

If the action seems too slow or completely ineffective—especially on coarse rasps and burrs—you can add hydrochloric acid. You can find this at your home improvement center under the name "muriatic acid." It's typically used for cleaning mortar residue from bricks. THIS IS A DANGEROUS CHEMICAL— READ AND UNDERSTAND ALL CAUTIONS ON THE LABEL. Add it slowly to the toilet bowl cleaner—NEVER ADD CLEANER TO THE ACID; A DANGEROUS REACTION COULD OCCUR. I've found that a 50/50 mixture is maximum strength. With more than that you could wind up with a smooth surface rather than sharpened ridges.

Architectural Carving: Techniques for Power & Hand Tools

Once the tool is restored, I rinse it thoroughly, dry it, and immediately coat it with oil. If it's not oiled it will rust with atmospheric moisture very quickly.

That rusty rasp that started my experiments? I still have and use her. She ain't pretty but she's a lady.

POWER SHARPENING

It is not my intent under this heading to belittle any power sharpening system on the market today. Some seem to be very good, but I have used none of them—only seen them demonstrated, and I must confess that I'm not overly impressed. Here I'm going to tell you how I do it—a method that has been years in the development. My system does require several power tools, but these can be had for a minimum investment.

Grinder

Very handy to have for tool maintenance is a grinder. This need not be a super-heavy-duty, industrial model but merely a small, inexpensive, ½-horsepower, machine will suffice (4-27). If you don't have a wheel dresser (to the immediate right of the grinder in 4-27), you have only half a grinder. Grinding wheels can become out of round; the corners can wear off; gullies can form in the center of the wheel. More important, wheels can become clogged with metal particles (4-28). When holding the wheel dresser firmly against the grinder's table (4-29), the cutters of the wheel dresser spin and bounce, breaking up the surface of the wheel, restoring its shape and removing any clogging.

If the cutters of your wheel dresser get to looking like those in 4-27, buy a replacement set (far right, 4-27). These are often shipped coated with a sticky rust preventative. Be sure to clean the "sticky" from the cutters before installing them; they must spin freely.

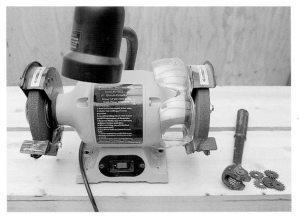

4-27 A small grinder is necessary for tool maintenance.

4-28 Grinding wheels can become clogged with metal particles.

4-29 A wheel dresser in use.

71

SAFETY WITH A GRINDER

Never use a grinder without safety glasses. Don't rely on that cute little flip-down plastic window that comes with many grinders (you'll note that I've removed the plastic windows from my grinder). Unlike wood shavings that can often be whisked from the eye, metal fragments and grit from a grinder are often hot and tend to stick to the eyeball. You will be making an emergency trip to your friendly neighborhood ophthalmologist. The experience is painful and expensive. Been there, done that . . . more than once I'm ashamed to say.

I keep a pair of safety glasses hanging on the grinder. If I turn the machine on without putting on the glasses, the vibration causes them to fall to the floor. This provides me with a small penance: I have to bend over to pick them up. As my back has an aversion to bending, I've formed the habit of putting on the glasses before turning on my grinder.

One other piece of safety equipment you might want to consider is a dust mask. I rarely use one if I'm only going to spend a few seconds touching up a tool, but if I'm going to spend any extended period of time at the grinder, I always wear one. While most of the particles of steel and grit are heavy and fall to the floor, there are also very fine particles, which float a bit. After spending five minutes at the grinder, take off your dust mask, look at it, and you will see why you're wearing it.

Tools can be easily damaged with a grinder. It goes without saying that they can be ground out of shape through lack of care, but overheating is a more common problem. As you grind a tool it becomes warm due to friction. If it becomes so warm that it turns blue, the hardness of the tool's edge is lost. You can check with a file to confirm any loss of hardness in blue areas. Sometimes it's not as bad as you may think. If the hardness is lost you have two choices. You can either carefully grind the blue area away or you can retemper the tool. (There is a sidebar on retempering, page 55, in the section on pneumatic chisels in Chapter 3). Neither is fun.

To prevent overheating, don't force the tool into the wheel. Rather, let the grinder just "kiss" the tool. Use a delicate touch. Keep a bucket of cold water handy and cool the tool frequently. Don't just dip the tool then go back to grinding; swish it in the water until all of it becomes cool to the touch. I often place a saturated piece of paper towel near the cutting edge **(4-30)**. This not only helps keep the tool cool but also the water starting to boil alerts me that the tool is becoming too warm. In all cases, be very careful when grinding near the corners of the tool where the metal has little bulk to absorb the heat.

4-30 A water-saturated paper towel can be used to prevent overheating.

Should I have occasion to grind inside the channel of a gouge—perhaps to alter the sweep slightly—I use a tapered stone powered by a drill or die grinder **(4-31)**. This ensures that the curve will remain true, for oftentimes I use a gouge to cut circles. This is hard to do if the sweep is not true.

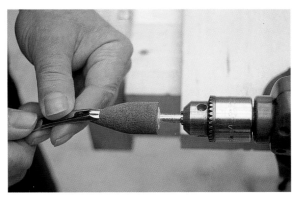

4-31 A tapered stone can be used to grind the channel of a gouge accurately.

4-33 Belt sanders used in the first step of polishing.

My grinder is equipped with two wheels, one about 80-grit and the other about 120-grit. The coarser wheel cuts quickly and the danger of overheating is not as great as with a finer wheel.

If I am grinding a tool to remove nicks or reshape it, I grind all the way to the edge, using the coarse wheel. If I am just restoring a bevel that has become blunt through wear, I only grind to within about $\frac{1}{32}$-inch of the edge (4-32). That way I don't have to polish out any heavy scratches left by the 80-grit.

4-32 Grind tools only near the edge to eliminate repolishing.

Belt Sander

Once I have done the heavy work on the grinder, I move on to a belt sander.

I use a type that takes a 1-inch belt (4-33, left). Belts are readily available and come in a good assortment of grits. Any clogging is easy to remove by holding a wheel dresser against the moving belt. It also breaks up the grit, sharpening it and making it somewhat finer.

In lieu of the 1-inch belt sander, you can use a regular belt sander (4-33, right). I'm fortunate that my sander rests comfortably on my bench. If yours doesn't, come up with a method of gently clamping it to prevent your chasing it all over your bench.

The sander constitutes the first stage in polishing. I use the finest belts I can find, 320-grit. That is a rather coarse grit for a polishing operation, but I save belts that have the grit almost worn off of them and these do provide for an even finer cut. There have been times when I used an old cold chisel on a new belt to break up the grit and hopefully make it finer.

As with the grinder, there is a danger of overheating the tool. Don't lean on it. Use a delicate touch, letting the tool barely contact the moving sandpaper. And be sure to have that container of cold water on hand to cool the tools.

I mentioned above that many of my tools have a slightly curved bevel. This is accomplished by holding the tool over an unsupported part of the belt. I don't use guides with the sander but rather judge the angle by the distance the butt of the handle is held from the running belt or a particular spot on the bench.

73

Power Stropping

When the tool comes from the belt sander, it will have some fine metal particles hanging from the edge (4-34). These will be removed in the polishing or stropping process.

Polishing in the channel of a gouge is what I find most challenging. Here I usually start with a small rubber wheel, impregnated with diamond dust, powered by a motor tool or a die grinder (4-35). The motor tool is better, in that its speed can be adjusted to a slower rate.

After the diamond wheel I switch to a stiff felt wheel with jeweler's rouge applied to it. This can be either an actual wheel or a cone-shaped felt device (4-36).

To polish the bevel you can use a cloth wheel mounted on your grinder. I say you could, but I don't recommend it. It will polish, but it will also tend to round over the edge due to its softness. A better choice would be a stiff felt wheel or even a disk cut from MDF (medium-density fiberboard).

The above technique describes the method I used to use. If you'll thumb ahead to Chapter 19 in Section IV, "Useful Tools & Equipment You Can Build," I describe how I do it today.

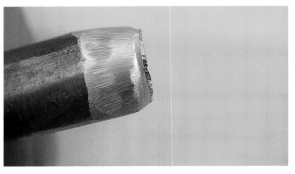

4-34 Particles left after grinding.

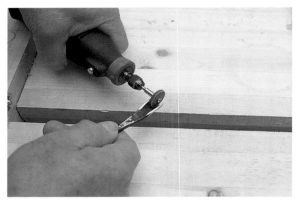

4-35 The channel of gouges can be polished with a diamond-impregnated rubber wheel.

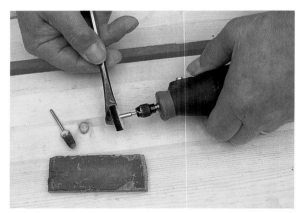

4-36 Further polishing can be done with a felt wheel loaded with jeweler's rouge.

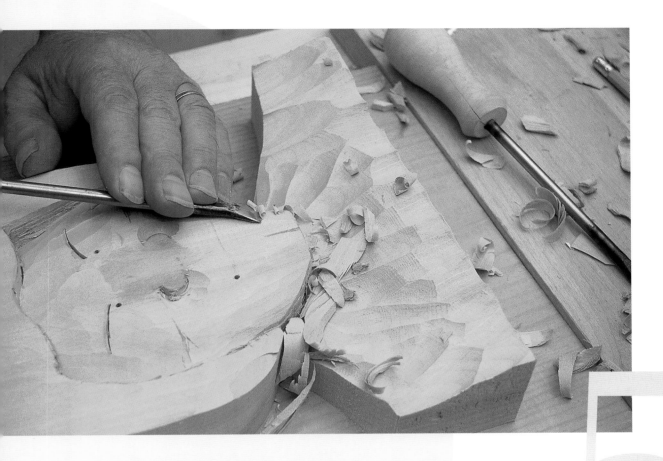

WOODS FOR CARVING

5

When you carve embellishments to be attached to buildings, you won't always have a choice of woods to work with. Too often you'll be stuck carving in the species that was chosen for the general woodwork in the building. Nevertheless, some woods are more suitable for certain things than others. So if you can have any say in the matter, you ought to know what woods are available and which would be a good choice for architectural carving.

HARDWOODS

Technically speaking, a hardwood is any wood that comes from a deciduous tree, that is, a tree with leaves that fall. That makes balsa—that soft, lightweight stuff they make model airplanes from—a hardwood. The "hard" in hardwood has nothing to do with the wood's durability. Balsa, of course is very lightweight and very soft, while long-leaf yellow pine—which is a softwood—is quite dense, heavy, and harder than the back of your head. Try explaining the foregoing to a hardheaded client.

If the architect's specifications say only that the embellishments be carved from hardwood, my first choice would be **basswood**—also called linden and limewood, of the genus *Tilia*. This close-grained hardwood is rather soft and cuts very well with sharp tools. It is a complete pleasure to work with. In many cases you find a mallet completely unnecessary.

Second on my list would be **mahogany**. This open-grained hardwood is also a pleasure to work with. I don't care for that stuff from the Philippine Islands, which I don't consider a true mahogany, but rather the lumber from Africa or South America. While Philippine "mahogany" (genus *Eschweilera*) cuts easily, its stringy, coarse nature makes fine detail difficult. The African (genus *Khaya*) and South American (genus *Swietenia*) varieties are finer in texture. As it is somewhat harder than basswood, you'll find yourself using a mallet with mahogany, but final smoothing cuts are easily made by hand.

I once carved a frame to house a seven-foot-by-ten-foot mirror. The whole thing was so large that the glass people fastened the mirror to the wall, then the carpenters mounted the frame over it with the aid of a forklift. The client was unconcerned with the type of wood since the frame was to receive a rather opaque finish. Though it was substantially more expensive than other woods on hand, I chose mahogany. The ease with which it works well made up for the additional cost.

While the frame was in progress, the client decided that it would be a shame to cover the mahogany with paint, so a natural finished was specified. I proceeded to do much smoother work. By the time the frame was ready for the finishing shop, the client decided that gold and silver leaf was the only way to go. I cringed—wanted to cry.

The story does have a happy ending. My son Christopher, who applied the leaf, packed it tightly into the open grain with a stiff brush. Then, once a dark glaze was applied to accentuate the grain and residual tool marks, both smiled beautifully from beneath the gold and silver leaf.

When selecting mahogany, avoid boards and planks with a ribbon figure—that's the figure seen on so many 1930s mahogany tabletops. The grain changes dramatically from one side of the ribbon to the other, and the fibers in the ribbon stand almost straight up but in scattered disarray. You might also want to select softer boards and planks. Lift the material. The lighter will be the softer.

Architect's specifications are not usually vague. Some years ago **oak** seemed to be the wood of choice for interiors. Oak (genus *Quercus*) is definitely not my favorite wood for carving. Its hard nature gives the mallet a real workout, and I usually use blunter tools to prevent nicks. It seems that every time I have some fine detail in a design, it winds up in a coarse open-grained area of the board.

If you must carve in oak and your work is in areas that won't receive close scrutiny, consider substituting **butternut**. This wood (*Juglans cinera*) is much softer and the grain is somewhat finer, although from a distance it looks very much like oak.

Ash (genus *Fraxinus*) is another good oak substitute, and sometimes it is used by itself in interior woodwork. This is a tricky wood, for in a unit of ash you'll find pieces that are very hard and dense. In that same unit there will be pieces as soft and light as bass. Choose your material well.

I think my strongest objection to oak, butternut, and the like of open-grained woods lies in that coarse grain. If the work is given a slightly dark finish that accentuates the grain—which is usually the case—any detail in the carving disappears in the grain (5-1).

Today, *maple* seems to be in vogue. Maple (genus *Acer*) is every bit as hard as oak, but its close grain makes fine detail a snap. Oh yes, the mallet will get a workout and blunter tools are in order when working in maple, but the wood cuts clean and tools move through it smoothly.

When selecting maple boards and planks, look for vertical grain. That knurly stuff from the base of the tree and near large crotches is almost impossible to work with. I always specify twelve-foot lengths. Boards and planks of that length are usually cut from more choice logs taken from a little higher in the tree.

If you are working for the more opulent, you might find yourself working with *walnut* and *cherry*. Banks in my area are particularly fond of walnut (genus *Juglans*). Both woods are moderately hard but carve well. Cherry (*Prunus serotina*) presents a little challenge in that it's "sticky"—I'll discuss that below. And you will find knurly boards and planks in both species. You will also find pitch pockets, especially in cherry. Unlike in pine (genus *Pinus*), the pitch will be dry and will not ooze, but it always seems to wind up in areas of fine detail. Select your material well.

Economy as well as conservation come into play in many projects. Were I to receive a commission to carve some walnut brackets to be mounted ten feet off of the floor, they would be carved in *poplar*. When this light-colored—almost white—wood (genus *Populus*) is given a light coat of transparent orange dye then stained a walnut color, it is very difficult to distinguish from walnut, especially at a distance. There is no sense in using what is becoming a rare species when it's not necessary. There are green areas in

5-1 Heavy grain can hide the fine detail of a carving.

poplar. The green will turn a warm brown with exposure to light and air.

Poplar is moderately soft in texture and carves well. Like cherry it also is a bit sticky, but that can be dealt with.

If there are talented painters on the job, they can turn **alder** (genus *Alnus*) into a number of species, especially if the work is to be viewed from a distance. With the proper stains, it can look like walnut or mahogany. If the painters add a few streaks, pin knots, and sap pockets, it can look very much like cherry.

Alder carves quite easily—almost as well as bass. As the alder tree is not huge, you will encounter knots and "wows" in the grain where it approached a crotch. Alder is excellent for small projects, and it is cheap enough that defects can be discarded.

SOFTWOODS

I suppose that the most common species of softwood in the lumber store is **pine** (genus *Pinus*). This wonderfully soft wood carves very well, though tools must be razor sharp to carve it cleanly. The resins in the wood lubricate those tools and they glide almost effortlessly through the project. Oh the wonderful odor of those resins. A pine project leaves my shop smelling like all outdoors for weeks. I hate to sweep the floor and throw away all of that wonderful smell.

Those resins can also pose a challenge in that they can form surprise pitch pockets. These pockets will, of course, be found in the most inopportune places—Murphy's Law. Don't cry. Simply cut them out and plug the hole.

Like other species, pine trees have limbs and in profusion. Knots are very common. But pine trees can grow to be very large and some are carefully pruned, so you will find plenty of boards and planks that are almost perfectly clear and straight grained—but these are also "perfectly" expensive.

A TRICK FOR SOFT-TEXTURED WOODS

Carvers in the Southwest prefer to work in pine. If that is not to your liking, they can use pine. And if that won't work, they can execute your commission in some very choice pine. While basswood carves cleaner than pine, it is also more expensive. Poplar and alder compare in price but they tend to be "sticky." That is, the tools tend to stick to the wood and do not glide through it as easily as the resinous pine. Cherry is also a very sticky wood—the worst I can think of.

Now there are some things that pine is just not suitable for. When you can get Southwest carvers to work in one of the sticky specie, they have one little trick that you should be aware of: They douse the work in kerosene. It is a wonderful lubricant. It also takes months to evaporate to where a good surface finish can be applied to the work.

As I don't usually have the luxury of months between working and finishing, I substitute turpentine or paint thinner (mineral sprits) for the kerosene. I prefer the turpentine, as it smells better. After placing a fan in the window near my workbench to carry away the fumes, I brush on the thinner and let it soak in for a few minutes before making final smoothing cuts. The thinner will usually evaporate overnight.

As you carve architectural embellishments there is another softwood you will encounter, **fir** (genus *Abies*, the true firs). This strong, durable softwood finds its way to the beams in open-beam ceilings, and those beams need brackets to support them. Fir is an absolutely miserable wood to carve in, especially if there is any detail required. The sapwood of this species is very soft—sometimes softer than pine—and it's like trying to carve a roll of paper towels. The heartwood on the other hand is harder than maple. Carving through

78

these transitions of textures can be challenging. When carving, try to carve with the transitions rather than across them (**5-2** and **5-3**). Carving across the transitions will leave a washboard surface.

5-2 **Carve with texture transitions.**

5-3 **Carving across texture transitions.**

NOTES ON GLUING

Wouldn't it be wonderful if trees grew 16 feet in diameter and about 300 feet tall—with no limbs? We would have nothing but perfect lumber any size we wanted. As such is not the case, we usually find ourselves building the sizes we need. This is usually done by gluing smaller pieces together to form our blanks.

In general woodworking you can get away with a lot of sloppy gluing and jointing. A small void in a glue line will often go unnoticed. In a blank for carving, a void can be

A TRICK FOR HARD-TEXTURED WOODS

Oak, maple, and some ash present a challenge in that they are very hard. Making those final smoothing-cuts can use up a lot of muscle. There is one law of nature that can help: water softens wood. When I find myself expending more muscle than I care to—particularly on end grain—I brush on a little water and let it soak in for a few minutes before making those final cuts. On end grain the process can be overdone. If the work gets too wet, the tool will pull fibers up leaving tiny holes in the work. Before using water, do a little experimenting, and don't experiment on your project.

disastrous. You might cut away all that is around it, leaving only the void exposed.

Grain matching is also important, but in gluing carving blanks, grain matching is a little different. In gluing up a tabletop you would want to select boards whose grain is all similar so that when joined they would appear as one. This is not so important in carving blanks, as the design of the carving will break up even rather dramatic changes in appearance. It is often more important to see that the grain or fibers of the wood are all running in the same direction to avoid grain changes that can interfere with carving.

To check the direction of the fibers I run my hand over the face of the board or plank in question. In one direction, it will drag; in the other, it will flow freely—much the same as running your hand over a cat's back. I often mark the boards as to the direction of the grain and the face tested, so that I won't get them mixed up in the gluing operation (**5-4**).

The components of any glue-up should also fit well. The face of planks in **5-4** were passed over a jointer to ensure they were straight and flat. There were absolutely no gaps at the ends.

Woods for Carving

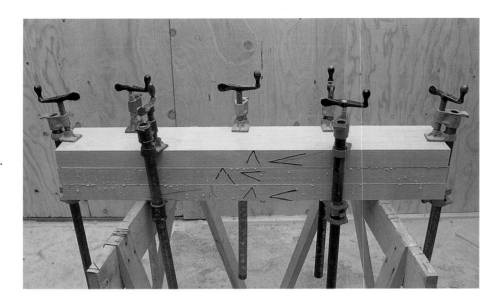

5-4 Planks marked as to grain direction.

When I glue up panels, I try to join the boards so that they are tight on the ends and slightly open at the middle—about $\frac{1}{16}$ inch in 4 feet—making what is called a "spring joint" **(5-5)**. Wood usually shrinks from the ends first. The pressure exerted by the spring joint pulls the ends together so that they won't check through this shrinkage.

Another important thing to consider is an even and sufficient spread of glue. A paint roller works best for me. So that I don't have to clean the roller after use, I keep it in a plastic container with a tight-fitting lid. About $\frac{1}{2}$ inch of glue on the bottom of the container acts as a glue reservoir and keeps the roller soft. If you use the roller daily, the glue will remain fresh. If you use it weekly, you may have to add a teaspoon or two of water to restore the glue's viscosity. I also add some fresh glue along with the water.

Some glues contain a biocide to prevent spoilage. This biocide is very sensitive to metal, especially zinc that is used in galvanizing roller handles. It will turn glue stored for any length of time to thin bubble

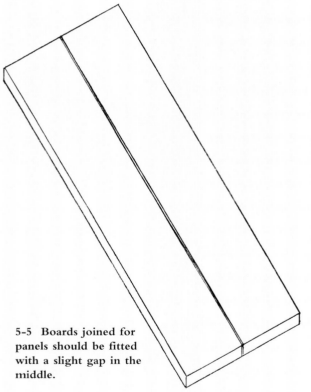

5-5 Boards joined for panels should be fitted with a slight gap in the middle.

gum. I therefore use a small roller with a plastic handle. The roller is more useful with a full-sized sleeve. The sleeve can be slipped

Architectural Carving: Techniques for Power & Hand Tools

80

5-6 Adding bulk to a small roller.

over the plastic roller's sleeve but it will be a bit sloppy. A bit of twine acts as a shim **(5-6)**.

I usually spread both items to be joined. I've learned to gauge the thickness of the spread so that there is a small amount of squeeze-out **(5-7)**. This indicates that the spread is sufficient. If the squeeze-out drips onto the floor, the spread is far too heavy. Glue might not be terribly expensive, but the glue on the floor sticks only to the floor.

5-7 Proper squeeze-out.

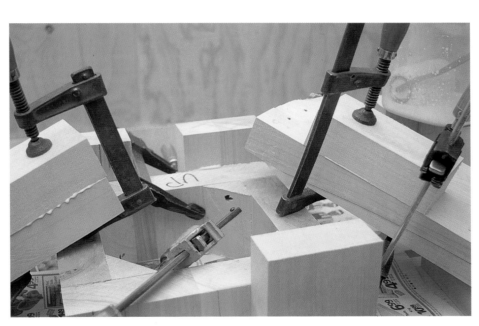

PART II

LAYOUT, CARVING & FINISHING TECHNIQUES

WORKING WITH PATTERNS, PHOTOGRAPHY & MODELS

I've always wanted to ask an impressionistic artist if that's what he or she intended to do at the beginning. I once did. Studying an alabaster sculpture, I noticed the artist standing beside me.

"Is that what you started out to do?"

"Sir, that is what I found in the stone."

"And what did you find in the stone?"

"That, sir, is a horse."

"Ahhhh yes, I see it now. Yes, very good, very good. Well done."

He walked away with a "Humph."

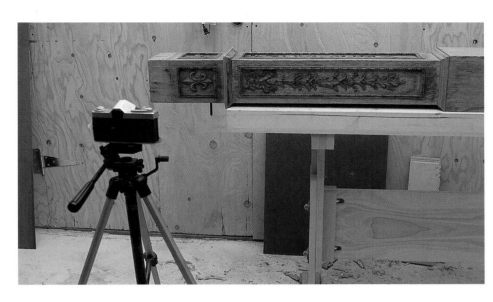

6-1 Photographing the subject.

Well, I'm sorry if I offended the fellow at the art showing, but it seems to me that before you start any carving project, it's a makes some sense to have an idea of where you're going.

WORKING WITH PATTERNS

My son Nick takes an interesting approach to carving acanthus leaves. He makes three or four flowing lines on the work then begins to chop away. In a few minutes out pops the leaf with the lines in the center. He says that the lines tell him where not to cut. Well, he's been carving acanthus leaves for 20 years, so I guess he can see them in the wood before he starts.

I have not usually been blessed with the opportunity to free-form anything. Rather, I am usually presented with a drawing, a photo, or an actual "thing" to duplicate. I, therefore, am forced to take a more precise approach. I have found that more often than not my clients will critically compare my finished work to the specifications.

Drawings and photos can be taken to a copy machine and enlarged or reduced to provide a paper pattern of the finished work—a little interpretation might be done along the way.

These can then be transferred to the work by means of transfer paper or cutting and outlining—pretty straightforward. Sometimes the above process can be a little impractical. For these instances, I employ other means.

WORKING WITH PHOTOGRAPHY

For precision, and in many cases ease, I have leaned on photography for my patterns. It's really quite simple. I photograph the subject in black and white (6-1) then project the negative and derive my pattern (6-2).

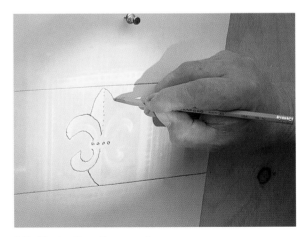

6-2 Projecting the negative.

85

Working with Patterns, Photography & Models

I've found that mounting the negatives in slide mounts is more convenient than working with the film alone. These slides can be placed in a slide projector for further ease.

Slide projectors do not have the most accurate of lenses and sometimes tend to be fuzzy. I, therefore, came up with a contrivance that holds the lens that I took the photo with, using the projector as a light source only (6-3).

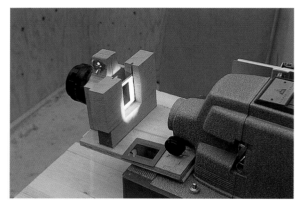

6-3 Setup for using the lens that took the picture to project it.

Now this may sound like the long way around, but not necessarily. The object being photographed earlier in 6-1 is a newel post. It is from the bottom of the stairway; the upper newel was destroyed in a fire. The character being projected is rather simple and could have really been sketched. Beneath that, however, is a labyrinth of twisted leaves that would have taken hours to sketch accurately. Since this was a restoration project and the client was already fighting with the insurance company, I didn't want to take a chance on spillover wrath. In addition, it's likely that the client would be able to view the reproduction sitting directly beside the original before installation. Separated by a flight of stairs comparison is difficult, side by side it's not so difficult. Besides, why try to develop your own artwork when you can copy someone else's.

You can, of course, shoot color-positive slides of the subject that you want to duplicate, but I often find the color distracting. Besides, a roll of black-and-white film is far less expensive to process. As a matter of fact, I process my own film. That way I can shoot only a couple of shots, then remove the exposed film from the camera—in total darkness—and process the few shots. If you're thinking that photography might meet some of your challenges, look into doing your own processing. It's economical and very simple.

WORKING WITH MODELS

Whenever possible, work with a model. If you're carving flowers or leaves, have some on hand (6-4). If you can't find what you need on a stroll through the park or garden, craft stores have an abundance of silk and dried foliage—don't get caught cutting a section out of your neighbor's grapevine. Even if you don't intend to carve a true and accurate reproduction of the plants, it will give you a point to stylize from.

6-4 Various floral models.

If it's an animal you intend to carve, have the appropriate animal on hand (6-5). Do this, of course, by means of figurines—horses, chickens, and the like are messy and don't stand still long. My lady has a collection around the house that won't quit—figurines,

6-5 **Various animal models.**

The client wanted the same flow of lines. I used the flow of the foliage but couldn't quite see how I could depict the flowers in wood. Enter modeling clay. I am not much of a clay sculptor, so I won't go into any detail on its use, but you might want to thumb through the projects in Section III as I have used it there several times.

6-6 **Various human models.**

not horses and chickens. Thrift stores are a good place to look. Stores that cater to the ceramic craft often have cast-clay figures ready for glazing and firing. These can be fragile, but they are very economical.

If you are going to work with human or humanoid forms, have one handy (6-6). For full figure work I have a number of dolls—Ken and Barbie are my favorites. These don't help much with muscle definition, but at least I get the joints in the right places.

If you are going to carve linenfold, don't hesitate to fold some linen (6-7).

Models can be kept beside you for reference as you work, or, if they are exactly what you want, they can be photographed as described and patterns derived therefrom.

In the "Pair of Carved Panels Project" in Chapter 15, I photographed the stained-glass windows that the panels were to set beneath.

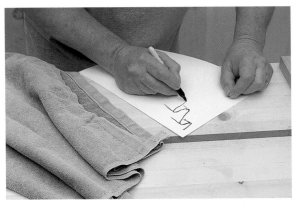

6-7 **A towel folded as a model for linenfold.**

87

Working with Patterns, Photography & Models

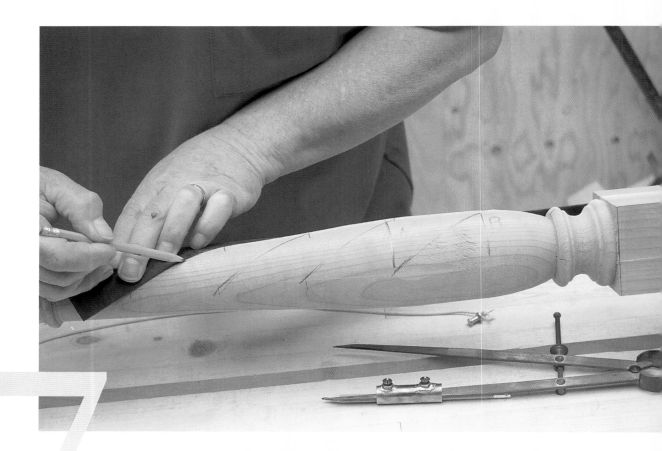

7

LAYOUT OF SPECIAL SHAPES

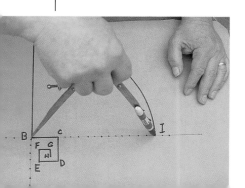

Transferring or marking out a design onto wood may require different techniques depending on the nature of the design. Making use of patterns, photography, and models is part of the basic approach, but some shapes require careful and precise yet practical methods in their creation. It is not my intention here to go into any lengthy discussion of geometry, but I would like to pass on some tips I've learned in dealing with the tricky stuff.

POLYGONS

Pentagons, hexagons, octagons, and the like can pose a challenge because of the angles at which their sides meet. I never concern myself with such angles, as I start with a circle. For instance, to determine the size of the segments of an octagonal glue-up for a column, I draw a circle the diameter of the column. After drawing a line through the center, I might even draw another perpendicular to the first. Then, beginning at the centerline, I walk a pair of dividers gently around the periphery. At the fourth step the dividers should meet the centerline at its other end. If they don't, I divide the error distance (7-1) by four and adjust the dividers and take another walk.

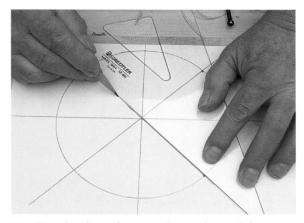

7-2 **Drawing lines from marks on the periphery through the center.**

7-1 **The error distance to be divided.**

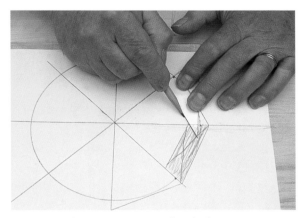

7-3 **Lines drawn tangent to the circle.**

Once I have half of the circle divided into four equal parts, I draw lines from the pinholes I made in the paper on my last walk through the center (7-2), thus dividing the periphery into eight equal parts. Then I can draw lines tangent to the circle that pass through the dividing lines and I have the dimensions of the segment (7-3).

It sounds like the long way around but it's the quickest and most accurate I've found with no math.

OVALS

Let me first state that two half-circles connected by straight lines is not an oval. It is a great shape for an "oval" dining table—gives more room and the challenge of getting the leaves to fit is eliminated. There are ways of drawing ovals with a number of circle segments, but there's math involved. I love math, but it makes my little head hurt. I use a different technique that comes from simple, but true, geometry.

Given the dimensions of the oval, draw line AB to equal its length. Draw line CD equal to the width, bisecting and perpendicular to AB. Call the intersection point E. From point C draw two arcs whose radius is equal to AE and intersect line AB (7-4). Drive nails or pushpins

89

Layout of Special Shapes

at these intersections and also at point C. Wrap a string around the pins and tie it securely **(7-5)**. (A piece of fine, flexible wire works even better as it won't stretch.) Then, pull the pin from point C, insert a pencil in the loop, and draw a true oval **(7-6)**. Ain't that clever?

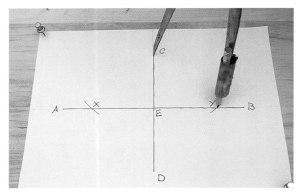

7-4 Lines drawn preparatory to drawing an oval.

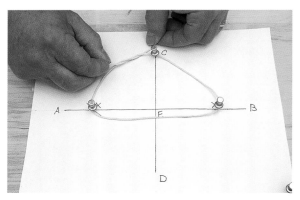

7-5 Preparing a string stretched around key points.

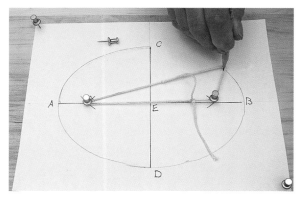

7-6 Drawing the oval.

SPIRALS & VOLUTES

To draw a spiral, drill a hole through a piece of paper and into a board. Stick a piece of string with a loop tied in the end of it into the hole. Remove the bit from the drill and stick it in the hole to hold the string. Place a pencil in the loop and draw a spiral **(7-7)**. As the pencil moves around the center, the string winds up on the armature. As that is a ¼-inch bit, the radius decreases at the rate of about ¾ inch per turn (¼ inch × 3.14). If you want it to decrease at the rate of ⅜ inch, use a ⅛-inch bit. If you want it to decrease at the rate of 1½ inch use a ½-inch bit. You get the idea . . . I hope.

7-7 Drawing a spiral by winding a string around a center armature.

This technique describes a spiral. That is, the circle decreases at a linear rate. Note that the lines are evenly spaced. More often you will want to draw a volute. Here the circle does not decrease at a linear rate. You could plot out some points around the spiral and do some freehanding, using the spiral as a guide **(7-8)**, but there is another way.

You could use a tapered armature in the center rather than a drill bit. In the case of **7-9** I've used the tip of a pencil. As the string winds around it, it winds around a decreasing diameter **(7-10)**. Changing the diameter of the armature as well as the taper can produce varying effects.

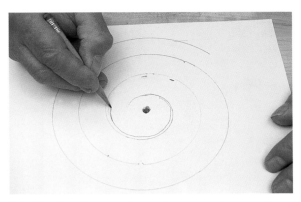

7-8 Freehanding a volute using a spiral as a guide.

7-9 Drawing a volute using a tapered armature.

7-10 String wound around the tapered armature.

There is yet another way, but this requires some math. Fear not, the math can be done with a calculator, the kind my kids and grandkids carry with them. I remember my grade school experiences and that nun with the flash cards. I remember how hard I had to work at learning my "numbers." Now all kids have to do is push buttons and record the results. I do have one advantage over the youth of today. When the batteries go dead, I can still function.

Knowing the size of the volute you want, draw a vertical line AB equal to its radius. Continue line AB down to twice its length. Draw line BC perpendicular and to the right of AB to equal one-fifth the length of AB. Lightly extend this line in both directions to match the length of AB. Draw line CD equal to 80 percent the length of BC, perpendicular to and below BC. Draw line DE to equal 80 percent of CD perpendicular and to the left of CD. You can continue in this manner until you run out of letters or paper, whichever comes first. We're only going to go to GH (7-11).

For all of the measurements I'm using a

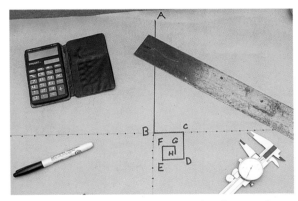

7-11 Lines drawn preparatory to drawing a volute.

metric caliper. It's much easier to read and set after all of these divisions. It's about the only use I've found for this caliper. It was on sale and in my greed I didn't notice that it was metric.

With B as the center and AB the radius, draw an arc from point A clockwise to the extension of line CD (7-12). Call that point I. With C as a center and CI the radius, draw an arc from I to the extension of AB. Call this point K. With D as a center and DK the radius,

91

Layout of Special Shapes

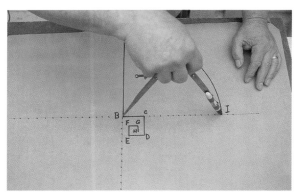

7-12 First step in drawing the volute.

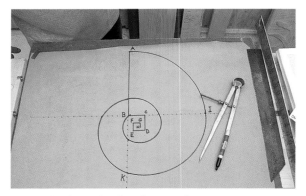

7-13 Final step in drawing a volute.

draw an arc from K to the extension of line CD. You don't have to call that point anything. I didn't; I got tired of naming points.

Continue from point "no name" in the above-described manner until you reach point H. You have now drawn a volute (7-13).

It may be that you want to carve a mold along the edge of your volute. If you want that line parallel to the edge, work as above with a starting center point B, but use BX as the radius. This will produce a parallel volute as shown with the arrow pointing to it (7-14).

If, on the other hand, you want a mold with a decreasing width, such as the other line, there is a little more division. Mark line BC at one-fourth of its length from B. Do likewise with CD, DE, etc. (7-15). Using the quarter mark on line BC as a center and the distance from that mark to X as a radius, draw an arc clockwise from X to the extension of BC. Continue drawing arcs using the quarter marks as centers and quadrant junctures as radii (7-16).

You will note that the second volute joins the first a little prematurely. Dividing the lines by one-eighth or one-tenth rather than one-fourth would have produced better results, but it doesn't show well in a photo.

By adjusting the division of AB and percentage of BC, CD, etc., you can come up with an infinite supply of volutes. I highly rec-

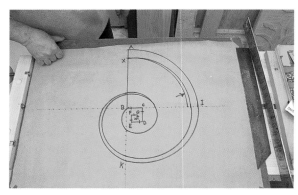

7-14 A parallel line to guide a mold can be drawn by starting at a different point.

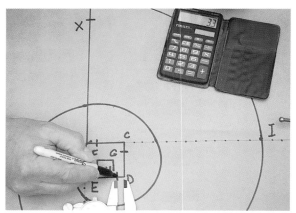

7-15 A decreasing-width line can be drawn by establishing different centers.

ommend that you draw volutes on as large a piece of paper as you can. Then, reduce them in size on a copy machine.

Architectural Carving: Techniques for Power & Hand Tools

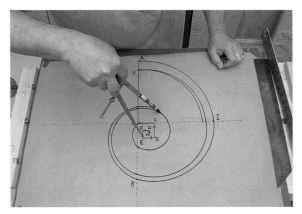

7-16 Using these centers the decreasing-width line can be drawn.

7-17 A template is made to draw both sides of a symmetrical design.

There is another and even more accurate way of drawing volutes. I'm not going to describe it, as it involves a circle, 18 lines, 40-some points, and would eat up several pages. It is the method that highway engineers use to design those cute decreasing-radius freeway on-ramps, the kind you find yourself going too fast on as you reach the end. The above will get you started.

Other Items with Decreasing Dimensions

While we are on the subject of decreasing dimensions, let's try one more. This is to be a stylized foliage with a small leaf at the tip and increasingly larger leaves down the stem. There are to be two such patterns meeting in the center, forming a symmetrical design.

First I make a template of the stem and draw both sides to get an idea of size and flow (7-17). Next, I walk a pair of dividers down one stem, tightening the dividers one-quarter turn with each step (7-18). After freehanding some lines to indicate the centerline of each leaf (7-19), I mark the tips, again using the template (7-20). Using the dividers again, I mark the width of each leaf, tightening one-quarter turn with each progressive leaf (7-21).

7-18 Dividers are walked down the stem, decreasing their width slightly with each step.

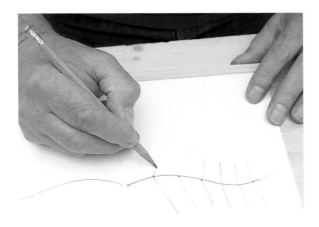

7-19 Lines are freehanded to establish the center of each leaf.

Layout of Special Shapes

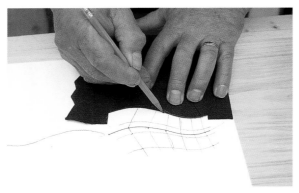

7-20 The tips are marked using the template.

7-22 The leaves are drawn within the given established points.

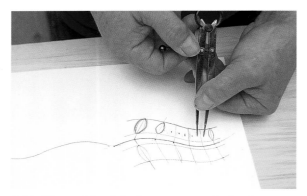

7-21 The width of the leaves are marked using dividers and decreasing their setting.

7-23 Patterns can be transferred using a household iron.

It's then a matter of drawing in the leaves with the given points (7-22).

Now if you will excuse me for a moment, I'm going to run up to my office and make a copy of this on tracing paper so that I can copy both sides of the design. I also want to make a couple of adjustments. Don't go away; I'll be right back.

Now it just so happens that my copy/fax machine prints with a heat-transfer process. If heat will put the design on the paper, heat will take it off. I pin the pattern to the board I'm going to carve and fire up my household iron to the high setting (7-23).

This little trick will also work with laser copies. Make sure you make them as dark as possible. Make one copy for each transfer you intend. Sometimes you can get two or three transfers per copy, but rarely. Also make sure that your board is smooth and free of dust.

SPIRAL REEDS

Round objects and turnings are always more eye-catching when reeded. Spiral reeding is especially attractive. Through the Southwest, you will see pine logs with spiral reeds used as columns. (Somewhere in the Southwest there is a machine that will cut spirals on those 10-, 12-, and 14-inch logs and it must be one hel . . . of a machine, but I can't say that I like the finished product. I would prefer to view and study the tool marks and the irregularity of the man's hand.) I have carved spiral reeds in pine lodge poles to be used as newels in rustic handrails. They are very attractive.

To lay out these spiral reeds I stretch my air hose diagonally across the floor of my studio at the pitch of the spiral I want. (I want you to pay strict attention to this demonstration. I went to a lot of work for it. I had to sweep the floor.) It is then a matter of rubbing chalk on the air hose and rolling the item to be reeded over the hose, keeping it parallel with the adjacent wall **(7-24)**. After a parting cut is made down this initial line, lines for the other parting cuts can be laid out with dividers. I'll show you how in Chapter 11, "Carving in the Round."

If the round you're working with has a square top or bottom, you can't very well roll it on the floor, but you can wrap a stout piece of paper about 2 inches wide around it at the desired pitch **(7-25)**. This will work provided that the round is of equal diameter throughout. If it is at all tapered, the pitch will vary with the taper **(7-26)**. This might be your desired effect. If so, go for it. If not, there is an approach that will keep the pitch uniform.

Define a point at each end of the round at the exact top. You can eyeball that exact top. It's not critical, but be as accurate as you can. Draw a chalked string between these points and flip a line **(7-27)**.

7-24 A spiral can be marked by rolling the work over a chalked hose or rope.

7-26 The pitch of a spiral will vary on tapered work.

7-25 A spiral can be marked by wrapping the work with stout paper.

7-27 A chalk line can be used to establish a straight line on irregular work.

Layout of Special Shapes

Next, divide the diameter of each end by four starting at the chalked line. Do this by wrapping a piece of paper around the round and mark the intersection **(7-28)**. If the round is severely tapered and the paper won't lie flat, divide an adjacent character **(7-29)**. Divide the paper by folding it twice, then mark the round **(7-29)**. Chalk three more lines to divide the round into quadrants.

In one quadrant, draw a line at the desired pitch **(7-30)**. Construct lines A and B parallel with the axis of the turning at the ends of the line you just drew—sanding scratches in the turning can be a guide. Set a pair of dividers to the distance between line A and line B. Mark out each chalked line with this setting. Then draw lines between the marks made by the dividers **(7-31)**. Repeat for each quadrant.

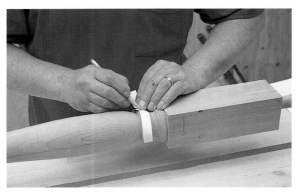

7-28 A piece of paper is used to divide the circumference.

7-30 A line is drawn in one quadrant at the desired pitch.

7-29 If the paper won't lie flat, an adjacent character is marked.

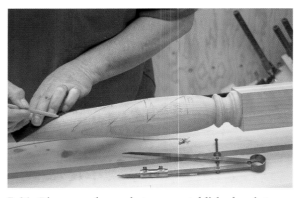

7-31 Lines are drawn between established points.

Architectural Carving: Techniques for Power & Hand Tools

SAFETY PRECAUTIONS FOR WOODCARVERS

8

I want you to know that I consider myself an authority on safety

. . . and I have the scars to prove it. I must say that all of my

injuries—save one—were due to my lack of attention, lack of

planning, and just plain carelessness. I was stupid and paid for it

in a very painful manner. I must also say that I have been lucky.

But being a student of odds and probabilities, I advise you not to

trust in your luck where assorted body parts are concerned.

Before we take tool in hand, it is duly incumbent upon me to add some specific notes on safety. It will make me feel better. It will make my publisher feel better, and both of our lawyers will be somewhat relieved.

Here I'll not get into chain saws, table saws, jointers, angle grinders, and the like. These are pretty scary power tools and usually get the respect they are due. I want to mention some of the subtleties of safety with regard to tools that don't usually get respect.

SAFETY

First and foremost on the list: Never push or drive a hand tool toward any body part. Consider that you are working on a bench that is about navel high. Were a razor-sharp tool, being pushed with considerable force, to slip, it could cause a life-threatening injury. Am I trying to scare you? No, I'm trying to make you think.

This same rule holds true when operating power tools. Never place a body part—usually fingers—in the path of the blade. As you work with power tools—especially the band saw—think. Where would your hands go if the wood disappeared? I lost the tips of two fingers because of a disappearing piece of wood. Oftentimes when band-sawing, the blade will exit the work sooner than you think. It might hit a soft spot or a split and advance far more quickly than it had been. If a finger is in the path . . .

When band-sawing you may be tempted to clear chips from the table while the saw is running. Of course, the proper procedure would be to turn off the machine first. I usually don't go that far, but I do make sure that the blade is buried in the work and out of reach of my hand.

Even something as tame as a die grinder and burr can cause injury. That sharp burr running at 15,000 rpm can remove hide and flesh to the bone in one quick pass. Keep both hands on the tool, and don't wear loose-fitting cloth-

ing. That burr can wind a shirtfront up to your chin before you can let go of the trigger. How do I know that? I don't want to talk about it.

Even a gouge lying innocently on the bench can cause injury. Most of the little cuts and nicks I have received have been caused by coming into contact with the cutting edge of one tool as I reached for the handle of another. Keep your tools neatly placed on the bench, all aligned in the same direction (8-1). As you study some of the project photos in Part III, you'll note that this admonition is a "do as I say, not as I do," but I try . . . honest. When my bench becomes cluttered with tools that I'm not using, I stop for a moment and return a few to the wall. If there is a tool that I use rarely, I hang it up after use.

Some recommend that the cutting edges all face the edge of the bench for easy identification. I don't. Vibration from the mallet can cause those cutting edges to hang over the edge of the bench. And these, gentle reader, could produce some interesting scars about the midsection.

Never reach for a tool that is falling to the floor. I learned this lesson in my youth while working in the electronics industry. I saved a hot soldering iron from a terrible fall. The iron did not appreciate my heroism and rewarded me with a nasty burn. When you reach for

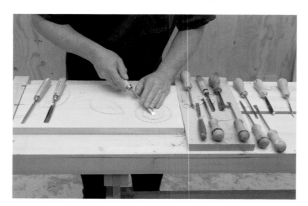

8-1 Tools should be neatly placed on the bench, all aligned in the same direction.

98

something falling, you are apt to do so quickly, and that speed can destroy your aim. Sometimes I will hold out the toe of my shoe to break the fall of a tool. I usually work above a concrete floor, and Murphy's 56th law of inevitability boldly states: "A gouge falling to a concrete floor will land on the weakest corner of its cutting edge." I can prove this by the nicks in the leather of the toe of my shoe.

Above I gave strict instructions never to push a tool toward any body parts. There is an exception. Note in **8-2** that the tool is aimed at the body of the user. Note also that the heels

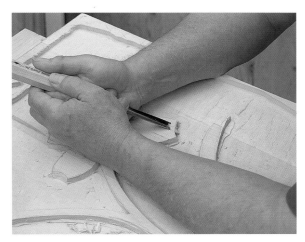

8-2 **With certain techniques, it can be safe to push a tool toward you.**

of both hands and even the forearms of the user are firmly contacting, or "anchored" to, the work. Should the tool slip, it will advance no farther than the hinge action of the fingers and wrist will allow, and this would not come close to reaching the body.

This concept of anchoring is very important to me and I even use it on the band saw. When sawing small pieces, I usually anchor the heels of both hands and push only with my thumbs. I anchor the heels in such a position that if the wood were to disappear, my thumbs would come nowhere near the blade.

Often when using a table saw or jointer, I let my hand ride the fence of the machine so that if the wood disappears my hand will rest on the fence, out of harm's way.

The concept of anchoring has posed a challenge to me. Perhaps that's because I anchor very firmly. Slivers and sharp edges of a design ravage the heel of my hand and the outside of my little finger. I usually get very involved in my work and don't notice the injury to my hand until I see tiny red marks appearing on my work. At this point I seek protection.

A glove is the obvious solution, but I don't like to work with gloves on. You can't feel with gloves on. I did meet this challenge to a point by taking a pair of scissors to an old glove, leaving only the little finger and a web for the thumb **(8-3)**. The duct tape? Those slivers and sharp edges also ravage the protector. When the duct tape becomes ravaged, it can be replaced.

8-3 **An old glove can be adapted to protect the heel of the hand.**

For even more freedom I made a "glove" from soft leather for my little finger only. The part that protects the heel of my hand and forearm fastens with strips with hook-and-loop on the ends **(8-4** and **8-5)**.

Safety Precautions for Woodcarvers

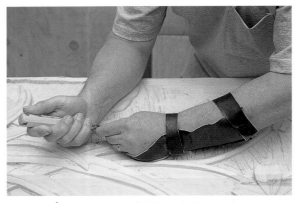

8-4 Protection can be fashioned for maximum freedom.

8-5 The little finger is protected and the forearm can endure extended anchoring on the work.

HAND POSITION

There must be some ultimately safe way to hold a tool, a way that will also lead to maximum control. In preparation for this section I did some research. I talked to woodcarvers. I read books. All I came up with was conflicting opinions. I started making notes of my hand position and found it changed dramatically with different operations. As you browse through the photos in this book, keep in mind that the hand position of the model is often posed to show the tool in addition to hands,

that position not necessarily being the best for the operation. The only common denominator I could come up with is that the tool is normally managed with both hands, one guiding and one pushing or driving with a mallet. If you have both hands on the tool, at least you can't cut your hands.

I was about ready to delete this whole section when I discovered the proper hand position for holding carving tools, and I discovered it in the most unlikely place, the grocery store.

As I stood in the checkout line, I made special note of the position of the hand of the young lady in front of me as she held her pen and wrote out a check. Later I tried holding a pen in that manner and found that I could not contort wrist or fingers into such a position.

I was taught in grade school that good penmanship could only occur if the pen were held in the "proper" position. Believe me, I learned that proper position. If my hand varied only two degrees from proper, there would be the deafening slap of a yardstick on my desk, and my hand would be bent those two degrees by a very large nun.

Now, one would think that the young lady, not holding her pen properly, would have poor penmanship. *Au contraire*, her penmanship was beautiful, exemplary. My penmanship is illegible. My signature can only be read by the scanner at the bank.

The moral? Hold your tools in a position that is comfortable and permits complete control for you. If another criticizes, smile, point to your beautiful work, and say, "Works for me."

I will only add that you should practice guiding the tool with either hand. I am somewhat ambidextrous and find that it saves me a great deal of moving around.

INCISED CARVING

9

A carving form in which the design lies below the background is called "incised carving." Incised means "cut in." Relief carving, on the other hand, has forms and figures projecting above the surface. All carving was once contained in the word "sculpture," which appeared in the fourteenth century from the Latin word for "to carve." Now we distinguish between carving in the round, also called sculpture, and carving that is set against a ground—relief and incised carving.

Embellishing architecture with carvings need not involve time-consuming projects requiring a vast assortment of tools. Less than thirty seconds, using a short-sweep gouge, can turn a rather uninteresting rosette to one sporting a flower (9-1). Only one tool required.

9-2 A saw can be used to make parting cuts.

9-1 Embellishments can be very simple.

CHIP CARVING

If a person were limited to chip carving alone, there is an infinite amount of decoration possible. Let's investigate some of the cuts possible.

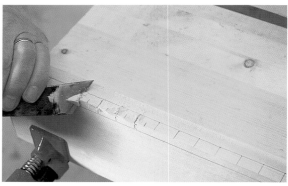

9-3 A cut is made from the center of the waste to the parting cut.

Try something with two tools. Clamp a board on edge and scribe a line down its approximate center. Scribe another line on the face the same distance from the edge. Lay out a number of evenly spaced lines perpendicular to the scribed lines. With a fine saw, cut along these lines to make parting cuts (9-2). You could make those parting cuts with a chisel, but it's likely you would chip out the material between them. The saw is just as quick.

From the center of the material between the parting cuts, with skew or chisel, cut to the bottom of the parting cut (9-3). Turn around and make the same cut in the opposite direction (9-4) and remove a triangular-shaped chip. You now have an edge decoration very popular in the Southwest motif. Just to keep it from getting monotonous, cut a few/skip a few (9-5).

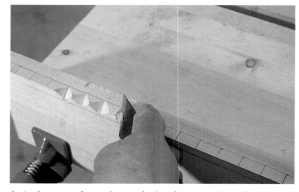

9-4 A second cut is made in the opposite direction.

How about something a little more daring with curved lines? Try a stylized fern so popular in Victorian embellishments. You'll need three tools for this operation if you want to count the knife.

Architectural Carving: Techniques for Power & Hand Tools

9-5 To avoid monotony, some characters are left uncut.

After transferring the pattern to the work, make a parting cut with a knife down the center of each leaf (9-6). (The pattern for this exercise was developed and transferred in Chpater 6 "Working with Patterns, Photography & Models.") This cut need not go all the way to the bottom of the finished design. It merely keeps the next cuts from chipping out at the extremities.

With a bull-nose gouge, cut along the outline of each leaf on one side toward the center (9-7). Come back and cut from the other side. If you don't use a bull-nose, you will find yourself overcutting at the extremities or leaving waste uncut in the center. There is a technique you can use with a straight gouge, and we'll talk about that in a bit. I do so much of this type of work that I have invested in the bull-nose.

Now, run a V tool between the leaves to depict the stem (9-8). With a little sandpaper clean away any residual pattern and you're done, less than three minutes (9-9). This is one design I've carved into a lot of door

9-6 Parting cuts can be made with a knife.

9-7 A bull-nose gouge is used to cut from the line to the parting cut.

103

Incised Carving

9-8 A V tool depicts the stem.

9-10 The skew will need to be tilted to make a complete cut.

9-9 Sandpaper is used to remove any pencil lines.

rails—very quick, very simple, but it adds that "something."

TRIANGULAR DESIGNS

Clamp a board on your bench and lay out some squares—about 1 inch. Draw some diagonal lines from corner to corner on each square. Sink the tip of a skew about $\frac{1}{8}$ inch deep at the intersection of each diagonal line. The skew's cutting edge will probably not reach the corner of the square, so tilt it forward so that a parting cut is made to the corner of the square (9-10).

Next, I prefer to let the tip of a skew ride along the parting cut to the bottom or center of the chip. Then I swing it forward with its edge following the line of the square until it meets the adjacent parting cut. In instances

where I'm cutting with the grain, I make two cuts, the first to check the grain (9-11). If the chip removed tends to flow downward toward the opposite stop cut, I work in the opposite direction.

You might find it more convenient to remove the chips with a chisel (9-12). Sometimes I do too. Just be sure you have a chisel wide enough to make the cut in one pass. (You'll note in 9-12 that I'm cutting against the grain. How is that possible? That chisel is very sharp.)

You may find it difficult at first to hold whatever tool at the correct angle to remove all the chips to the same depth. There's no law against having some guide on the bench to help you. An angle square works fine (9-13). If someone walks into your studio, casually tip it over. I won't tell what you were using it for.

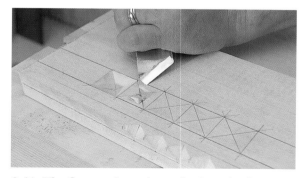

9-11 The first cut is made to check grain direction.

Architectural Carving: Techniques for Power & Hand Tools

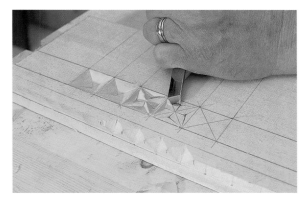

9-12 A chisel can also be used.

9-14 Bullets are carved with only two cuts.

9-13 An angle square can be used to guide the tool at the proper angle.

DESIGNS WITH CURVES

Chips need not all be triangular. Make a few stop cuts with a gouge. Then come back and make a cut into the stop cut. You now have a border design that the folks in the Southwest call "bullets" (9-14). Note the slightly bull-nosed gouge to the right in 9-14. That is what I use to make the stop cuts; it fits to the bottom without overcutting in the corners. It won't work for the chip cut though, as it won't reach the corners.

Are you getting bored with borders? Lets try something a little different.

As chip carving lends itself to Celtic-type designs, we'll lay one out that looks like a bunch of flower petals. Make a knife stop-cut

through the center of each petal. Cut lightly at the tips of the petal and lean on the knife at the center (9-15). Unless you lean on the knife very heavily, it is unlikely it will reach the bottom of the intended chip, but that is unnecessary. The knife cut is primarily there to keep the design from tearing at the tips, much the same as in the stylized fern.

9-15 A knife is used to make this parting cut.

Hold a narrow-sweep gouge at an angle and slide it into the center circle. Then while twisting the handle, push it around the periphery of the circle, removing a chip at the center of the design (9-16).

Push a large, shallow gouge to the center of the petal design. When the corners of the gouge reach the extremes of the design, tip the

105

Incised Carving

9-16 A gouge is used to remove a chip in the center of the design.

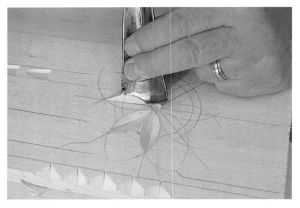

9-17 The corner of the gouge is used to reach the center of the parting cut.

9-18 A V tool is used to outline each petal.

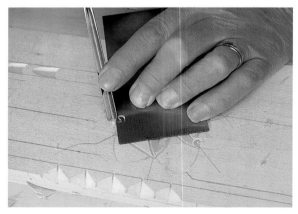

9-19 The V tool with a guide is used to cut a straight line from tip to tip of each petal.

gouge to one side and slip the corner through the cut, hopefully reaching the bottom and center of the design (9-17). Here I'm using a square gouge rather than the bull-nose used above in the stylized fern. If you overcut slightly at the center, it is of no great moment. Now, push the gouge in from the other side of the petal, again tipping and pulling the corner through the bottom of the design. If all has gone well, you will remove a single chip. If there is residue left on the other side, go back and clean it up with the corner of the gouge.

This can be done with a narrower gouge by tipping it and letting the cutting edge follow the line while the corner strives for the center and bottom of the cut. You may have to make several attempts from both sides. This is an example of the most convenient tool for the job. Carrying that idea one step further, if I had a lot of this design to carve, I would grind a bull-nose gouge that would fit to the bottom of the design as I did in the fern above—no tipping required.

With a *sharp* V tool, outline each petal (9-18). Don't worry about any material that might not be completely severed at the outer tip, because in the next step you are going to make a V cut from tip to tip of each petal (9-19). Yes, it is acceptable to use a guide for

106

Architectural Carving: Techniques for Power & Hand Tools

the V tool. Just make sure that it's wide enough to hold firmly without endangering your hand should you slip.

Outline the whole design by placing it in a square cut with the V tool. Cut a triangular chip design in each corner of the square. Then pervert the concept of chip carving a little by texturing that little patch that's left **(9-20)**.

I've only carved one quadrant so far; you can finish the other three.

9-21 **Three circles are drawn to depict various parts of the flower.**

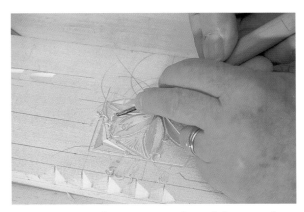

9-20 **A very-small-sweep gouge is used for texturing.**

A STYLIZED SUNFLOWER

Before we leave incised carving, let's try something a little more elaborate and perhaps something more useful. Rather than giving instructions, I'll tell you how I attacked this project.

I first acquired a model. In this case I chose a silk sunflower. I studied the flower for a time and decided that I would stylize a bit, as I had no intention of portraying all of those petals. I noted the dome in the center of the flower containing the seeds. Then I noted two distinct lengths of petal, some short in a distinct circle and the longer ones reaching to the periphery of the flower.

With the aid of a compass I then drew three circles **(9-21)**, one depicting the dome, one for the short petals, and one for the periphery.

I then drew a curved line from the flower to represent the stem. Yes, I know that sunflowers have straight stems, but straight lines are not always visually attractive. Let's just imagine a large gorilla stepped on this plant when it was very young.

Next I drew in two leaves. As long as I had the model I drew the actual leaf **(9-22)**. No sense in trusting in my poor drawing ability.

9-22 **A model is used to draw the leaves.**

Using a V tool I lightly set in all of the pencil lines with the exception of the circles that would be the flower. In the case of the stem I had drawn only one line. After setting that in, I marked the other side with a pair of dividers

107

Incised Carving

so that the lines of the stem would be parallel **(9-23)**. For the stems going to the leaves I used a tighter setting for the dividers.

About this time my daughter walked in the studio and asked what I was doing. After I explained, she said, "Oh, Dad, can I have that when you're done? I can mount it by the stove to hang my pot holders on." After I agreed to give her the finished project, she said, "You know, it would be really sharp if I had a mirror of this one for the other side of the stove. I could hang those beautiful, wonderful, precious, special wooden spoons you made me on it."

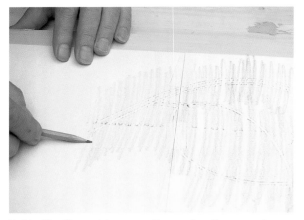

9-24 Shading with a pencil transfers lines cut in the wood to paper.

9-23 Dividers are used to mark parallel lines.

Flattery doesn't usually work with me, but from my daughter it always does. I prepared a pattern for a mirror image by placing a piece of paper over the outlined project and shading it with a pencil **(9-24)**. After placing this on some transfer paper—with the transfer side up—and running a pencil over the lines on the face, I had a mirror-image pattern for the other carving **(9-25)**.

After that little distraction, I went to work setting in **(9-26)** and rounding off the dome in the center of the flower **(9-27)**. Am I doing this wrong? Shouldn't I start on the outside of the flower? You'll see the reason in the next few steps.

Next, I set in the tips of the inner petals **(9-28)**. With that done, I hollowed out the

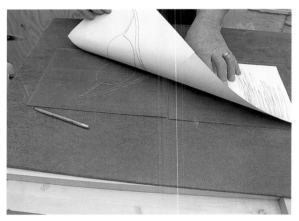

9-25 Drawing over the design placed on a piece or transfer paper creates a mirror image.

9-26 The design is set in.

Architectural Carving: Techniques for Power & Hand Tools

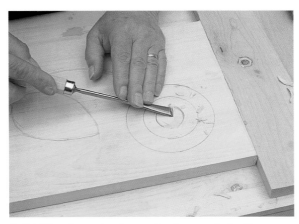

9-27 The dome in the center is rounded off.

9-28 The tips of the inner petals are set in.

9-29 Each petal is carefully hollowed out.

inside of each petal with the same gouge (9-29). You will note that the material removed from the dome area permits me to make all of these hollowing cuts easily. That is why it was worked first.

You will also note a dark patch in the lower left of the flower. That is a wet spot. I overcut a petal, through poor planning ahead, as I neared the end of the circle. I put a few drops of water in the overcut to swell it together. By the time I'm finished, you'll have a hard time finding it.

I worked the outer petals in the same manner, again using the same gouge for hollowing as the one used for setting in. Before I started I drew some arrows on the project. These tell me which direction or sequence to cut in. As the gouge cuts diagonally across the grain, one side cuts smoothly and the other tends to tear (9-30, tip of the pencil). Cutting in the proper sequence, the second cut cleans up the tear left from the first.

9-30 One side of a gouge cuts smoothly while the other tends to tear.

There were some fibers in tight spots that refused to part using the gouge, and these were taken care of with a small chisel (9-31).

As I was working, the tip of one of the inner petals fell off. I didn't slip. Honest. But I did put a tiny bit of glue under the errant piece and set it back in place (9-32).

Incised Carving

9-31 Tight spots are parted with a chisel.

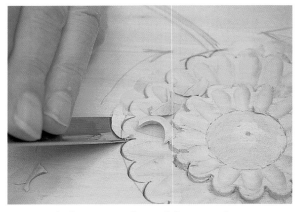

9-33 A shallow gouge is used for texturing.

9-32 Glue is used to replace pieces accidentally chipped out.

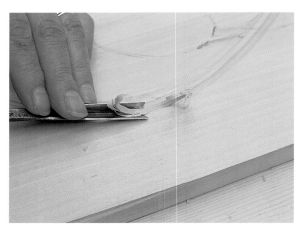

9-34 A V tool is tipped for special effect.

The last step on the flower was to cut in the periphery. Wanting a little texture around the petals to accentuate them, I recruited a shallow gouge for the task **(9–33)**.

By this time I was tired of gouges, so I picked up my trusty V tool and went to work on the stems. For this operation, I tipped the V tool so that the stem would stand almost perpendicular and there would be a wider sweeping surface to meet it **(9–34)**.

I then went to work setting in the leaves. For this task, I chose two chisels with slightly different widths **(9–35)**. I suppose that I could have set in that ragged edge with a V tool, but then all of the cuts would have been of equal length.

9-35 Chisels of different widths are used on the outline of the flower.

Architectural Carving: Techniques for Power & Hand Tools

110

I thought the two different lengths more pleasing. You will also note that the number of cuts is nowhere near as many as on the model. Realism is nice, but speed and ease is nicer.

To finish outlining the leaves, I used a shallow gouge (9-36). The fishtail pattern of the gouge made getting into the tight places a snap.

9-36 A shallow fishtail gouge is used to finish the outlining.

I was delighted to see that the veins of the sunflower leaf were recessed; usually, they stand above a leaf. With model close at hand, I sketched in the veins (9-37). Then I cut in each vein deeply with a V tool (9-38). With a skew, I rounded the leaf into each vein (9-39). There were some flat areas left, and these I hollowed with a shallow gouge to leave a flowing and irregular surface (9-40).

9-37 The center veins are sketched.

9-38 The center veins are cut deeply with a V tool.

9-39 A skew is used to round the leaf into the vein.

9-40 A shallow gouge is used to hollow portions of the leaf.

111

Incised Carving

Rather than trying to round off the stem with any kind of tool, I made several passes over it with a stiff piece of sandpaper **(9-41)**.

You probably have noticed in the preceding photos a certain fuzziness around the design, a few standing fibers that defied cutting. No, it's not due to dull tools; it just happens, and I don't worry about it. The last thing I do on any project is sweep away those defiant fibers with a small brass-bristle brush **(9-42)**.

And now for the finished product **(9-43)**. I'll carve the mirror of it when this book is safely in the hands of the printer.

9-41 Sandpaper is used to round off this stem.

9-42 Small, uncut fibers are disposed of with a stiff brush.

9-43 The finished product.

RELIEF CARVING

Unlike in incised carving, in relief carving the design stands out from the background rather than being cut into it. Forms and figures project above the surface. Working with the design itself is much the same as for incised carving, the removal of the background being the challenge. I will take you through one quick example of a relief carving to give you an idea of the sequence of events and the tools that are used for this form of architectural carving.

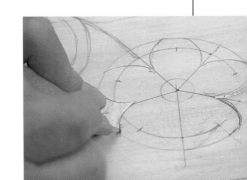

Once more, we're going to do a stylized flower. I can't really tell you just what kind of flower it is. I took the design from an old catalogue of architectural fixtures.

Here again I'm going to start with a circle the approximate size of the flower. This I divide into five equal parts **(10-1)**. After sketching the intersection of two of the five petals, I went over the lines with a V tool and transferred the marks to a piece of paper **(10-2)**. After cutting the intersection from the paper, I drew in the remaining petals **(10-3)** along with another circle to show the limits of the petals. I also sketched in a stem and a couple of rough leaves, but we'll get to those in a bit.

10-3 A paper pattern is used to assist in drawing the petals.

The first step in a relief carving is usually setting in the design. That is, going around it with gouges and chisels, making plunging cuts along the lines, perpendicular to the surface **(10-4)**. I intend this design to stand about ¼ inch above the background, and in the soft basswood that I'm using, I could drive a gouge the whole ¼ inch. But, trying to go the whole distance could apply too much pressure to the design, weakening it. I try for ⅛ inch at a time.

The next step is to go around the design with a shallow gouge, removing some of the waste **(10-5)**. After this is done, it's another trip around the design, cutting down the remaining ⅛ inch, together with another trip with the shallow gouge to remove some waste.

10-1 The circle is divided into five equal parts.

10-2 V-tool marks are transferred to paper.

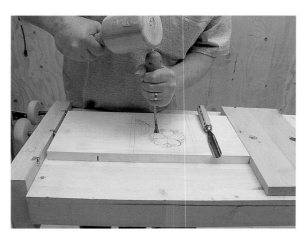

10-4 The design is set in.

Architectural Carving: Techniques for Power & Hand Tools

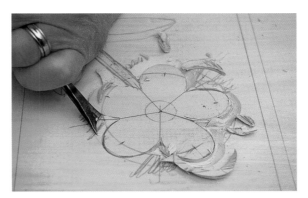

10-5 The design is outlined with a shallow gouge.

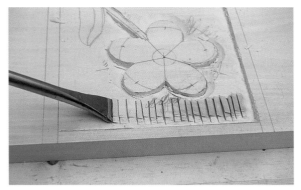

10-6 For grounding, angular cuts are made with a chisel.

If you are very careful, remembering that a narrow tool drives deeper than a wide one with the same strength of mallet blow, you can cut to a constant depth all around the design. Be careful not to overcut. There may be instances where you might wish to alter the design slightly by making it smaller. If you overcut, there will be a gouge mark left in the background. If you undercut slightly, you can always walk a gouge around the design by hand to cut away the waste, going the desired depth only.

Making a study of relief carvings, you may note that they stand about 3/32 inch above the background. This is particularly true of furniture embellishments. The depth is one mallet blow down, the quickest way to get some sort of a design on the piece.

Be sure that gouges and chisels you use fit the design and that the plunging cuts you make overlap slightly. You want the vertical surfaces of the design to be as clean and neat as possible. If you work carefully at this stage, you won't have to go around the design again to clean it up.

Next comes the removal of the background, sometimes referred to as "grounding." You can do this most accurately by making a number of cuts with a chisel (10-6), making each mallet blow the same strength. Then,

removing the loosened material with a shallow gouge (10-7). This is much the same method a carpenter would use to mortise in a lock plate or hinge.

I say that you can use chisel and gouge to remove the background, but if you will excuse me for a moment, I'm going to drop a sharp bit in my router.

The router has the advantage of removing the background to a constant depth, to say nothing of the lesser amount of muscle required. Normally, when I ground a carving, I work freehand, and I'm looking through a pair of dusty, scratched safety glasses. I don't even try to cut right up to the lines of the design. Just how close I get to the lines is directly proportional to the number of cups of coffee I've consumed before the operation.

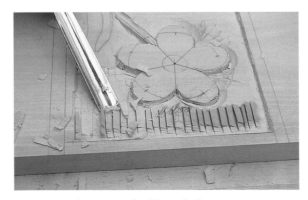

10-7 Waste is removed with a shallow gouge.

Of course the router won't do all of the work. There will be places that you have to resort to the chisel where the design gets close to the border and in the tight places between the petals **(10-8)**.

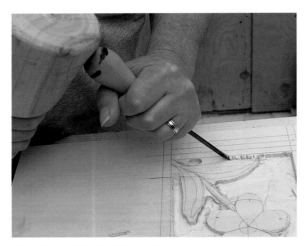

10-8 A small chisel is used to remove waste impossible to reach with a router.

I decided to give the leaves a little scallop to the edges. Rather than sketching, then finding the tools to fit, I used a tool to draw the sketch **(10-9)**. Anytime you get an opportunity to work like this, take it. If you are working with a limited number of tools, you might want to modify any patterns to fit your tools.

10-9 The design is drawn to fit the tools.

In any kind of relief carving a few bent tools will come in handy **(10-10)**. I can't tell you just how many times that bent, ⅛-inch chisel has saved me.

With the whole design set in, I sketch the folded-over tip of each petal **(10-11)**. I then made a stop cut around the center portion of the flower. For circles I'm partial to digging in one corner of the appropriate size gouge. Then, while twisting the handle, I push the dug-in corner forward with my thumb **(10-12)**.

To hollow out the center of the petals, I choose a narrow-sweep gouge. I really didn't have anything special in mind at the time, but the narrow gouge was there on the bench and it was sharp. As I worked, I liked the texture that the gouge left, so I dug out a spoon with the same sweep for the tight hollowing at the tip of the petal **(10-13)**, deciding to leave all tool marks.

At this point, I rounded off the center of the flower **(10-14)**. I had left it until now so that any slips in hollowing the petals would go into waste rather than the finished center character of the flower.

Next step: parting the petals **(10-15)**. In previous photos you might have noted that there is a ragged area between petals, especially those whose intersection runs diagonally across the grain. This is because the gouge that was used to hollow out the petals cuts with the grain on one side and against it on the other, tearing the delicate area at the intersection. Now this area is to be cut away. And with a tiny skew I did exactly that **(10-16)**, widening the parting cut and turning it into a V.

By this time I was really getting tired of that flower and wanted to move on to the leaves for a while, but I have to look professional. There was only one step left and that was to round off the tips of the petals with a shallow gouge **(10-17)**. In the process, I carefully blended the tips into the V cut, parting them.

Architectural Carving: Techniques for Power & Hand Tools

10-10 Waste in very tight spots is removed with bent tools.

10-13 A spoon is used on the tight portion of the petal.

10-11 Folded tips of the petals are sketched.

10-14 The center of the flower is rounded off.

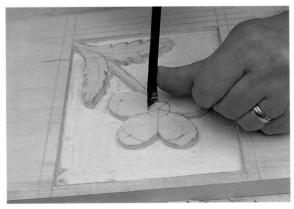

10-12 A circle is cut by pushing a gouge around the line with the thumb.

10-15 The petals are parted.

Relief Carving

10-16 A skew is used to widen the part of the petals.

10-17 The tips of the petals are rounded with a shallow gouge.

I still wanted to get to the leaves but decided to work my way down the stem with a shallow gouge (10-18). You'll note that I narrowed the stem in the process. You really didn't think I was going to leave that out-of-proportion stem, did you?

Ah, the leaves at last. After making a deep V cut down the center, I established the predominate plane of each with a chisel (10-19). It was then a matter of blending the outer edges into the deepened V cut with a chisel (10-20).

To finish off I put a vein in each leaf character with a small V tool (10-21). You'll note that I drew a pencil line for the veins before cutting them. Too many times I've become over-confident and messed up some good carving with poor veining. While these tiny veins are quite simple, my habit has become to draw first, cut second. You can always erase a pencil line.

The background was all that was left. It contained a lot of swirl marks left from the router. These could be attractive if they were more regular, but I have never found a way to make them regular. If I wanted to make the background perfectly smooth, I would use a scraper (10-22). I prefer a scraper with a gentle curve. I have others that are pointed for getting into tight places, such as between the petals. Sandpaper here is very time consuming and a general pain, especially getting into tight places.

You will see smooth backgrounds in furniture embellishment but not so much in architectural carving. Here you will usually encounter a textured background. One way to arrive at a textured background is with punches or stamps (10-23). Stamps can vary in texture and design and they are quick and attractive. Use them right over the swirl marks.

You can also texture with a gouge (10-24). In the lower area of 10-24 I've used a long-sweep gouge. The texture is barely noticeable. Above that I used a short-sweep gouge. The texture is much more pronounced. Above that I used a V tool. The deep V marks will cast quite a bit of shadow, making the background quite dark.

TEXTURING THE BACKGROUND

You can see in the photos some pencil lines scribbled on the background—a little trick. It can be difficult to see where you have been when texturing with a gouge. If you make some pencil lines on the background, when the lines are out, the texture is in.

Architectural Carving: Techniques for Power & Hand Tools

10-18 The stem is rounded with a shallow gouge.

10-21 A small V tool is used to put a vein in each leaf character.

10-19 The plain of the leaf is established with a chisel.

10-22 The background can be smoothed with a scraper.

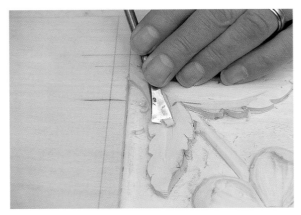

10-20 A chisel is used to blend the plane of the leaves into the center V cut.

10-23 Various stamps can be used to add texture to a background.

What possible application could such a carving have in architectural embellishment **(10–25)**? I once carved 40 of these flowers to be used as head-blocks for Victorian door casing.

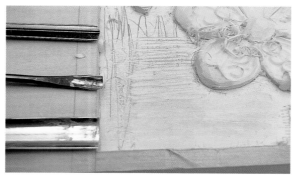

10-24 A gouge can be used to add texture to a background.

APPLIED CARVING

This little technique can save you a lot of time when carving several items in relief with a lot of flat background. Don't remove the background; apply the design. Band-saw your design in a thick piece of wood. You might need to clean up the edges of the design with rasp, riffler, or sandpaper. Then glue it to a substantial block of wood **(10–26)**. You can use a paper joint to make the block easier to clean up and reuse.

Mark the edge of the band-sawn piece to indicate the depth of the design **(10–27)**. Proceed to carve the detail on the face **(10–28)**. Then saw off the finished carving **(10–29)**. The carving can now be fastened to the background with glue or tiny brads.

10-25 The relief-carved flower showing a variety of ways the ground might be textured.

120

Architectural Carving: Techniques for Power & Hand Tools

10-26 A cutout design is glued to a scrap.

10-28 The face is carved and detailed.

10-27 A mark is made on the design to indicate the depth of the desired finished piece.

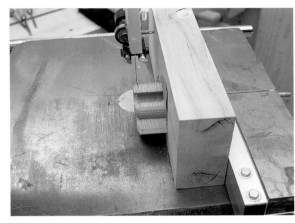

10-29 The finished carving is band-sawn from the assembly.

Relief Carving

1

CARVING IN THE ROUND

Until now, everything we have carved has been on a flat surface. It doesn't take long for this type of work to become boring unless you are working in very high relief. I must say that I prefer carving in the round—or at least 180 degrees of round. Perhaps I just like to work with large pieces of wood. Perhaps I just like the mind exercise of trying to envision the finished form in the blank.

CARVING SPIRAL REEDS

As long as I marked out a short log back in Chapter 7, "Layout of Special Shapes," let's work a portion of it to give you an idea of how to carve it.

I started by doing a little sketching on the bottom of the log. It seemed that four reeds would be attractive. I set my dividers for the spacing between the reeds **(11-1)**, then set them aside while I mounted the log in my vise.

11-1 Dividers are used to establish the spacing of the reeds.

The first step is to make a parting cut down the line made by the chalk and the air hose. You could use a handsaw with a piece of masking tape on it to mark the maximum depth of cut. As for myself, I'll use a small circular saw **(11-2)**. This is not the safest of operations. I would not consider it with a large machine, but I'm still "man enough" to hang on to a little 5¼-inch saw.

The line being cut is not exactly straight and the saw will tend to bind. To minimize this, I set the saw to cut to a depth of ¼ inch for a first cut, then made a second with the saw set to cut to a depth of just under ½ inch. The saw guard will interfere but it can be held back. At least that keeps both hands on the tool.

Using the parting cut as a guide I scribed more lines on the log for the other parting cuts, using the dividers set to the spacing back in **11-1**. The dividers should be held perpendicular to the parting cut **(11-3)**. My gray pencil didn't leave much of a mark, so I followed it with a piece of chalk.

11-2 A small circular saw can be used carefully to part the reeds.

11-3 Dividers should be held perpendicular to the parting cut.

After all of the parting cuts are made, you could use a wide chisel to make a stabbing cut at about 45 degrees into the parting cut to remove waste **(11-4)**. As for myself I'll resort to a wide chisel and my air hammer **(11-5)**.

My little circular saw left a rather wide kerf that I did not find attractive at all. I deepened the parting cut with a handsaw **(11-6)**. Note that I'm using a flexible handsaw that will

11-4 A wide chisel can be used to remove waste.

11-5 An air hammer takes the drudgery out of the task.

11-6 The parting cut can be deepened and trued with a handsaw.

bend to the slight curve of the cut rather than that back saw in **11-2**.

As a final step, I removed the heavy tool marks of the air chisel with a skew **(11-7)**. If you are carving something formal, sanding would be a final step, but enough of this log. Let's move on to something more challenging. Besides, that green log is rusting my tools.

11-7 Heavy tool marks are removed with a skew.

HOLDING THE FORM

Often you will find yourself carving brackets and such with acanthus leaves and scrolls that are really three designs carved on three surfaces and joined or flowing together at the corners. These are easy. Carving a form in the round— or half-round—can be a bit more challenging.

The first step is to draw a frontal view and a profile on your blank. (In this case, I chose a ram's head for the demonstration.) Then band-saw either the profile or the frontal. It's usually best to cut the easiest one first. Save the waste and tack or tape it back into place **(11-8)**. You'll note in **11-8** that I have cut the profile first. The large X's indicate waste that was left on so that I could mount the block in my vise. It will be cut off in the final stages.

The small arrows to the left indicate the direction of the two cuts I had to make in removing that piece of waste. The large arrows to the right indicate small areas that I left

124

Architectural Carving: Techniques for Power & Hand Tools

11-8 Waste from the first cutting is taped back in place.

11-9 Pieces are added to accommodate the design.

uncut. These areas will hold the waste in place until after the frontal is cut. It's just easier than having to tape them back in. After the frontal is cut they may be cut or broken off.

This particular block was not quite big enough to accommodate the horns, so I added thin pieces on each side of the head (11-9).

The next step is to draw some frontal and profile details on the sawn block. For the frontal, I referenced a centerline. Note the triangular holes in the drawing at the nose and forehead (11-10). These were used to locate the centerline before slipping in the transfer paper. For the profile, I referenced the back of the block. The block did not accommodate the drawing, but I saw nothing wrong with cutting the drawing to accommodate the block (11-11).

11-10 Windows are cut in the pattern to locate the centerline on the work.

SEEING THE FORM

There are those that can look into a rough block of wood and see the form. All they do is cut away anything that doesn't look like the form. These folks are truly blessed. I, Gentle Reader, am not so blessed. I have to rely on something other than instinct to do my carving in the round. That "something" is identifying and holding certain points of the form as I remove waste.

11-11 A drawing can be cut to accommodate the work.

Setting in the outline of the horn is rather easy and straightforward. At this point, it is set in on a planer surface. Determining the depth of the horn is another matter. It is easy to see that the back of the horn is the full width of the block. The base of the horn can be identified from the frontal view. It's the position of the tip of the horn that must be identified otherwise.

125

Carving in the Round

I make two black dots on the block, one indicating the position of the tip from the front and one indicating the position of the tip from the side. After removing all of the waste down to the one at the frontal view **(11-12)**, I can remove waste at the tip to that depth while maintaining the hard line at the outer edge of the horn **(11-13)**. With three points identified—the tip, the back, and the front— more waste can be removed and the plane of the horn established **(11-14)**. This procedure will also work with the front of the eyeball.

In any carving there will be times that you run out of distinct points from the pattern transfer on the block. These can be sketched in with careful measurements taken from the drawing **(11-15)**. Once the carving takes shape, it's just a matter of rounding things off **(11-16)** and adding detail—nostrils, eyelids, and so forth.

11-14 **The plain of the horn is established.**

11-15 **Details are sketched with measurements taken from the drawing.**

11-12 **Waste is removed down to the mark on the frontal view.**

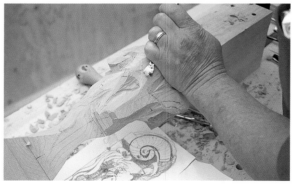

11-16 **The blocked form is rounded off and details added.**

11-13 **The hard line of the horn is maintained.**

Architectural Carving: Techniques for Power & Hand Tools

finish of the product.

PATCHING

I don't know about you, but I am not perfect. The material is not always perfect. I don't hesitate to fill small knots and such. There are times I make mistakes and I have no problem in applying a small amount of patching compound to a minor defect. Under certain circumstances, I have no problem applying a large amount of patching compound to a major defect. It all depends on the intended use and

For patching small defects, I am partial to nitrocellulose putty—wood patch, if you will. This is a wood-flour mixed with a binder. It comes in several colors to match several species of wood. It also absorbs stain much the same as the surrounding wood. As such, my patches are not readily visible. The material dries quickly, sands easily, and sticks moderately well. I therefore recommend it highly. I do not recommend it for areas that require durability. If you need durability, read on.

I must admit that in my early days I used to buy patch in large cans. Of course, then I was doing mostly cabinetwork and there were plenty of fastener holes to fill. As the years went by, I graduated to small cans of patch. Now I can't even get to the bottom of a small can without its drying out. Therefore, I keep a can of acetone on the shelf to thin it with.

today.

seem to fit the high-production needs of the techniques of the painters of old just don't

PREPARATION

No matter if you finish a project yourself or you ship it raw, it should be prepared for a finish. Believe me, no project-painter will pick up a piece of sandpaper to smooth someone else's work. Nor will they attend to any defect unless they caused it themselves. So many of

background on finishing products.

We'll talk about them right after we get the project ready for a finish and go through a minimal

PATCHING MAKES PERFECT

Often someone has pointed out one of my patches in an unfinished piece. I simply say, "Only the Almighty is perfect, and when we poor frail mortals approach perfection, the Almighty becomes quite unpleasant. With all of my problems, if you think I need Him on my case, think again. Why, that patch is a form of prayer, a sign of humility and repentance before He who has given us all things good, wholesome and lasting." As I speak, my voice increases in volume and I begin to project. If there is something handy to stand on or behind—such as a soapbox or pulpit—I take advantage of it. This usually quells further criticism and makes that everyone wish they had never pointed out the patch.

During my career I have had the opportunity to strip, study, and refinish many genuine antiques. The production of some of these pieces did not fall under the hands of a great carver but rather a master at patch and retouch.

I always seal the backsides of panels that are to become wainscot and such. The carpenters will never think of it and the painters won't be on the job yet. I also seal the backsides of brackets and the insides of hollow columns. I can't even imagine a painter with his arm down a hollow column. This little step can prevent the finished product from self-destructing over the years and should be highly considered.

If you do have a chance to finish your own work, you want to do it for maximum effect. If you have gone to the time and trouble to do a great carving job, there is no sense in hiding it with a poor finish. If you do your own finishing, there are two important techniques to remember always: Strikeout and glaze.

FINISHING FOR
MAXIMUM EFFECT

As an architectural carver, you will find that your work will often leave your studio in a raw or unfinished state. The finished product will be at the mercy of the painter on the project. Does that make you feel a bit helpless? There is one little trick that you can do to assist the painter. We'll talk about that when we get to the section "Sanding." In the meantime, there is some finishing I always do before any project leaves my studio. It's not seen but I feel that it's worthwhile.

(Some lacquer thinners will thin patch, but acetone works best. It dries quicker and has no other ingredients that can soften the patch.) Are my small cans of dried patch a source of pride, a means of bragging? You bet. It took me forty-plus years to get there.

For patching large defects, especially anything to be painted, I'm partial to auto-body putty. This material is filler mixed with a catalyzed resin. A catalyst is added just before use. It is very durable and sticks very well. It is often more durable than the wood itself.

I've discovered that there are two forms of auto-body putty. One is called surfacing putty. It has a large quantity of resin in proportion to the filler contained. It sticks very well, is very hard, and is very smooth in texture. The second type is a general-purpose putty. Though it sticks well, it is not as hard, as it contains less resin in relation to the filler. It's also coarser in texture.

Color is a challenge with auto-body fillers. The material itself is a gray color, but the catalyst comes in several colors to assist in mixing. These have no resemblance to wood tones. (I will mention that there is a similar product especially designed for patching wood and it is colored to wood tones. It is a good product but rather expensive for patching large areas.) The color challenge can be met somewhat by using the white catalyst and adding a small amount—less than two percent—of universal tinting color. The ultimate solution is a good touch-up artist.

In the "Door with Carved Panels Project" in Chapter 17, a clamp holding the router guide came loose unbeknownst to me and the router went awry. I am ashamed to say that I let the blankety-blank clamp come loose twice. The defects I patched with auto body **(12-1)**. When I assemble the door, I will make sure that the patched panel will be on the outside of the door, which will be painted.

12-1 Defects can be patched with auto-body putty.

In the "Pair of Column Capitals Project" in Chapter 16, the filler blocks that I added were not quite large enough. The little gaps left were also filled with body putty.

Body putty can be a bit tricky to use, but I have a procedure. I apply the putty and stand by until it sets firmly. Once firm the material is solid enough to cut with carving tools, and I do so at this point to rough the patch into shape. If the putty is left to cure thoroughly, it becomes harder than the back of your head, especially the surfacing type. After roughing the patch into shape, I then leave it to cure a couple of hours before attempting any sanding. Cured putty will not clog sandpaper, as the newly set putty will.

SANDING

Do you have to sand? Sanding is not my favorite activity. I like tool marks. It shows the "man's hand." Unfortunately my work is judged in comparison with manufactured products and these seldom bear tool marks. I find myself doing a lot of sanding.

There is another thing to consider. Tool marks made with super-sharp tools are very smooth, almost glossy, a thing for the carver to be proud of. Painters hate these glossy surfaces. They refer to them as "mill glaze." Stains sprayed or brushed on these areas tend to run

129

Finishing for Maximum Effect

and do not "take" or penetrate the wood. If you don't sand to remove tool marks, at least sand lightly to remove the mill glaze.

I mentioned above that there is a way that you can trick the painter into helping you accent your carving. This is done in the sanding step. I sand the whole carving with 120-grit paper. Any spots I want highlighted I sand with 220- or 380-grit sandpaper. These areas will hold far less stain, much the same as mill-glazed areas, but they will hold enough to please the painter.

If *you* sand the work, don't destroy the sharpness. Think twice/sand once. If you are sanding a leaf, say, sand the sides first. The paper will bend over onto the face, rounding off the edge. But then sand the face of the leaf, restoring the sharp edge.

STAINING

Stains can enhance a carving, but they should also enhance the wood. Heavily pigmented stains will darken the low spots of a carving enhancing the high spots. But they also hide the beauty and iridescence of the wood. Personally I avoid them at all costs.

There are also one-step finishes such as Danish oil and other colored penetrating oils, some with a small amount of pigment. Color is usually completely dependent on the absorption properties of the wood. Considering all of the grain changes in a carved piece, using these products can often lead to disaster.

If I am after a quick finish, I choose a wiping stain that is mostly dye with a slight amount of pigment. The dye colors the wood along with the pigment. As the stain is wiped off, a large amount of pigment is left in low spots, accenting the high spots of the carving. The slight amount of pigment left on the high spots will be minimal and can enhance the grain while not hiding the iridescence.

Generally, I prefer to work with dyes alone and gain the accent through a technique called

glazing that we'll discuss below. I spray the dye, and in this manner the wood is colored evenly. I am in complete control of the color and not at the mercy of the absorption properties of the wood. With this technique, I have complete control over not only the color but also the amount of accent.

TOPCOATS

Because of periodic cleaning of buildings and their embellishments, color and accent should be protected by a clear topcoat of some kind. There are so many topcoats to choose from and there is so much hype as to their properties that I would prefer to skip the subject entirely. But I will state my preferences briefly.

I have always been partial to nitrocellulose lacquer forced through the tip of a spray gun. It's quick to dry, quite durable, and compatible with all stains and glazes. True, it is not quite as durable as other products, but there is little contact with most embellishments other than in cleaning.

I avoid slow-drying varnishes of all types. The dust challenges are totally unnecessary. The only time I have used such a varnish is on a south-facing exterior door, and the type was spar varnish. Although it does yellow, it is remarkable stuff.

Environmental considerations in some localities have outlawed solvent-based chemical coatings. In these areas, such things as lacquer and spar varnish are out and you will be using a water-based product. I used to avoid these, but research in the past few years has brought water-based topcoats a long way. Though most are slightly milky, there are some very good water-based products on the market today.

GLAZE

The technique of glazing can best be defined as adding color selectively for the purpose of accent. The color is added with a heavy-bodied stain designed for the purpose. These stains are usually very slow drying so that you will have plenty of time to work with them.

I prefer to apply the stain with a brush **(12-2)**. That way I can pack the color into all of the tight, low spots. If puddles form I can pick them up with the tip of the brush.

For the accenting, I like to use the dry-brush method. That is picking up some of the glaze from the surface with a dry brush. The tip of the brush can be used to put some streaks in the remaining glaze, creating a little interest in an otherwise dull background **12-3)**. Keep a cloth handy to wipe the removed glaze from the brush.

The side of the brush can also be used to remove glaze from large areas **(12-4)**. Another effect is to remove all or most of the glaze from the surface, leaving it only in the low spots. This is best done with a cloth folded into a pad so that none of it will reach the low spots **(12-5)**. All of the glaze can be removed from the surface by dampening the pad with mineral spirits and turning it frequently.

Take a close look at **12-5**. Note the difference between the portion of the design with glaze—to the left—as compared to the portion without—to the right. Do I really have to point out which portion was glazed?

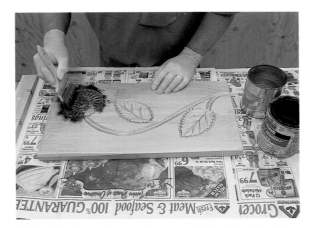

12-2 Glazing stains are best applied with a brush.

12-4 The side of a dry brush can be used to remove glaze from large areas.

12-3 The tip of a dry brush can be used to create interest.

12-5 A cloth pad can be used to remove glaze.

131

Finishing for Maximum Effect

STRIKEOUT

Another accent technique is called "strikeout." It involves removing color to achieve accent. A pseudo form of strikeout can be achieved by sanding all high spots with very fine sandpaper, preventing heavy penetration of stain in these areas.

After the piece has been stained—and the stain dried—strikeout can be accomplished by removing some of the stain with an abrasive pad or fine sandpaper **(12-6)**. On painted, "funky finishes" you can strike out some of the paint with a damp cloth before it dries **(12-7)**. (The project should be stained—if desired—and sealed before the application of the paint.) Or you can strike out after the paint is dry, using an abrasive pad lubricated with water **(12-8)**. (Flat paint strikes best. Gloss or semigloss tends to "ball up" and clog the pad.) Be sure to keep a damp cloth handy to clean up the removed paint and work carefully so as not to overdo. Cutting through the paint and into the sealer can cause grain-raising.

12-6 An abrasive pad can be used for strikeout.

12-7 A damp cloth can be used to strike out wet paint.

12-8 An abrasive pad lubricated with water, will strike out dry paint.

A COMBINATION OF GLAZE & STRIKEOUT

Glaze and strikeout can be used in combination and usually are found in funky finishes. Above, we struck out a painted panel, giving it the appearance of much wear through time and housecleaning, let's say. Now, imagine that the cleaning crew was not too thorough.

They got most of the grime but did not pay attention to the corners and tight places.

To simulate this condition, glaze is brushed into the low areas and smoothed out with a dry brush **(12-9)**. Then, with a cloth dampened with mineral spirits, residual glaze is scrubbed from the background so it won't alter the background color **(12-10)**.

12-9 Glaze is packed into low areas and smoothed with a dry brush.

133

12-10 A cloth is used to completely remove some glaze.

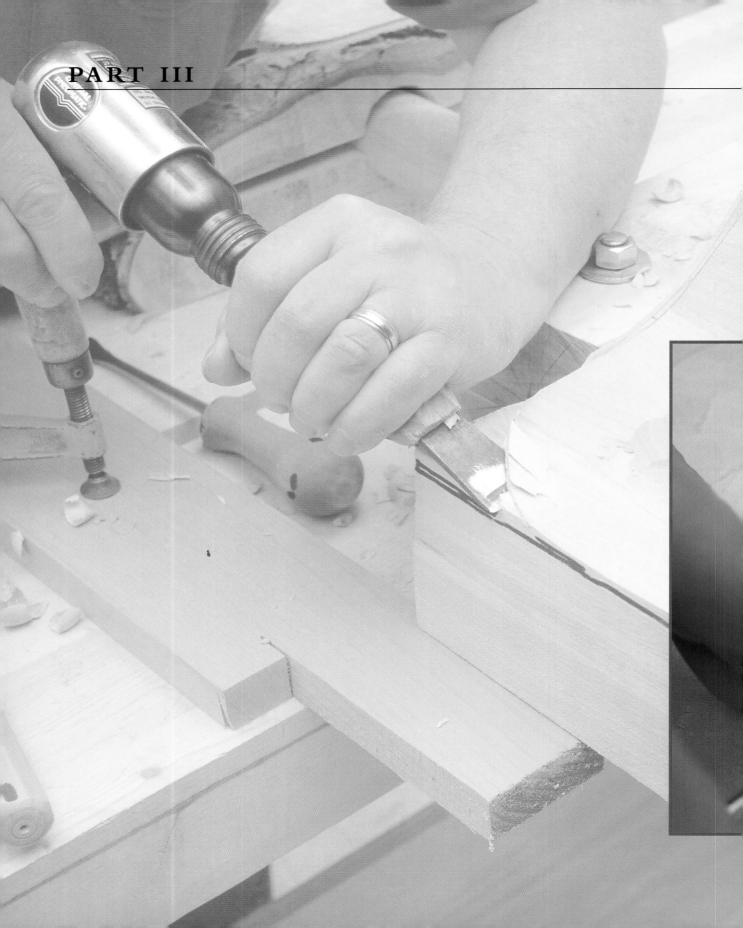

PART III

ARCHITECTURAL CARVING WITH POWER & HAND TOOLS

SET OF TOWEL BARS PROJECT

A charming young couple had a bedroom set made with carved door and drawer pulls. These were beautiful, two leaves, separated by about 6 inches, whose stems curled and formed the pull. They wanted matching towel bars for the adjoining master bathroom. The company that manufactured the drawer pulls did not, unfortunately, make matching towel bars. Enter the woodcarver and a commission to carve them.

Now, it might have been possible for the couple to buy some drawer pulls, cut them in the middle, and add a length of wood for the towel bar. This was not quite practical, though, as it would place the bar only one inch from the wall, and that's not quite enough room for a towel. Also, the leaves of the drawer pull would be a little out of proportion for a large towel bar. Their best option was to ask a woodcarver to create exactly what they wanted.

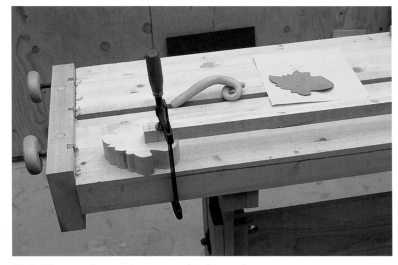

13-1 The rough-cut pieces are glued together.

LAYOUT

In order to place the towel bar itself far enough from the wall to hang a towel on it, the first plan was to have it dive steeply into the leaf and, after making one turn, it would become the leaf stem. After cutting out the leaves, and armed with a clay model to help me in positioning, I glued a stick to each one. The slide would become the bar (13-1).

The initial plan didn't work. The area of that steep dive was far too fragile and broke even as I was working. I tried gluing it back together, thinking I could reinforce the area with a dowel from the backside. Then I said, "No way." I decided to have the bar make two turns before becoming the leaf stem. I then crudely chopped out the other end of the broken blank to see how it would look.

As I worked on the model, I realized that marking all of the blanks was going to be a bit of a challenge but only a challenge. After rounding off the attached pieces (you'll note in 13-2 that I had to add an additional little piece adjacent to the bar) and cutting a little into the leaf (13-2), I wrapped a piece of string twice around the blank (13-3). With the string as a length measurement, I cut a piece of

13-2 The work is prepared for measuring.

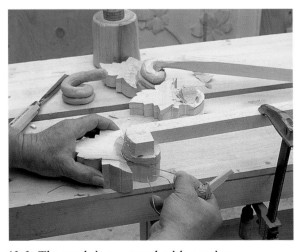

13-3 The work is measured with a string.

Set of Towel Bars Project

heavy paper that tapered from ¾ inch (the diameter of the bar) to ⅜ inch (the diameter of the stem as it joins the leaf).

I then used the paper to mark out the twisting, turning, and tapering bar as it turned into the leaf stem **(13-4)**. I darkened my pencil lines with a marker and, just to be sure that they all came out the same, I set them side by side **(13-5)**.

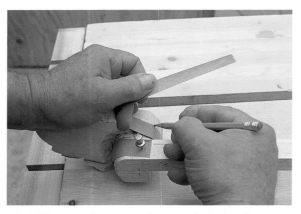

13-4 The template is used to mark the work.

138

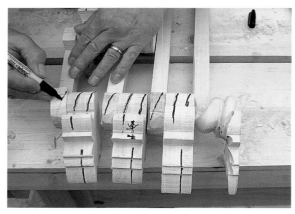

13-5 For accuracy, all of the pieces are compared.

PARTING THE TWIST

Using a chisel to part the twist was out of the question; it would work like a splitting wedge. In tight areas, I used a mini die grinder with a straight carbide burr **(13-6)**. Where I had room, I used a saw **(13-7)**. In

13-6 A mini die grinder is used to make parting cuts in tight places.

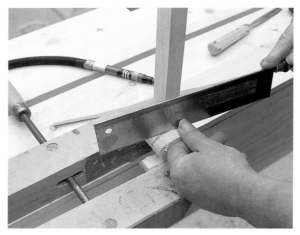

13-7 A saw is used to make parting cuts where space permits.

order to carry the parting operation to the bottom I had to remove the waste from the leaf **(13-8)**. I found the air chisel very handy for the hard maple. Cutting away from the twist, I worked with vigor. All cuts made toward the twist were made with extreme caution **(13-9)**.

One leaf tip was to cover part of the twist, so before continuing, I located and hollowed out the leaf tip **(13-10)**. Thereafter I continued parting the twist with my mini die grinder **(13-11)**.

Architectural Carving: Techniques for Power & Hand Tools

13-8 Waste is removed to permit carving the twist.

13-11 Parting is continued with the mini die grinder.

CARVING THE TWIST

End grain is not fun to carve, and half of that twist is end grain. Using only hand pressure, I began with a skew **(13-12)**. The skew quickly removed the large amounts of waste. In order to perfect the round surface, I switched to a gouge **(13-13)**. The parting cut made with the mini die grinder wandered a bit, but it was easily trued with a curved, triangular riffler **(13-14)**.

13-9 Because of grain direction, cutting toward the twist is done with caution.

13-12 The rounding of the twist is begun with a skew.

13-10 An overlapping leaf is located and roughed in.

13-13 A gouge aids in the rounding of the twist.

13-15 A riffler is used to refine the twist on the end grain.

13-14 A triangular riffler aids in truing the parting cut.

13-16 Stiff sandpaper is used to finalize the twist.

As you can see in the preceding photos, I didn't do too bad a job rounding things off, but some of the irregularities came out a little beyond the reach of sandpaper—particularly on the end grain. These were easily refined with a curved, flat riffler (13-15). I used that riffler with a very light touch, not wanting to scratch the wood any deeper than necessary.

From there, I took over with sandpaper. A strip of stiff sanding cloth did most of the work (13-16). And that triangular stick with the sandpaper glued to it to the right of the work in 13-16 took care of the very bottom of the part.

CARVING THE LEAF

The plane of the leaf flowed mostly away from the twist. I could reach only the tip with a conventional carving tool (13-17). I do have some spoons and curved gouges, but hey, this is the twenty-first century. I resorted to a die grinder and burr to shape the leaf (13-18).

Basically, each character around the periphery of the leaf is hollowed out, the hollow flowing to the center of the leaf and the twist. To prevent the ridges of all of these hollows from falling into the same plane, I shaped them with a gouge (13-19). Then I went back with the die grinder and sharpened each ridge.

The die grinder did not reach all the way to the twist. I was able to finish off the work with

13-17 Conventional tools can reach only the tip of the leaf.

13-18 A die grinder is used to shape the leaf.

13-19 Ridges between leaf elements are set in different planes with a gouge.

a gouge **(13-20)**. Here I found myself cutting slightly against the grain, but the distance was short and the cuts came out smooth.

Since I used extreme care with the die grinder in the final stages of shaping, I was able to use diamond rifflers for the final smoothing. Slight irregularities are often hard to see in maple, so I enlisted a flashlight to cast some shadow on things **(13-21)**.

13-20 Final shaping of the leaf toward the twist is done with a gouge.

13-21 A flashlight can be used to locate irregularities.

As a final step I ran a vein in the larger leaf segments. As each vein went through several grain changes, rather than using a V tool, I used the mini die grinder with a very small carbide burr **(13-22)**. Of course the veins came out slightly shaky and there were wood whiskers in either side. These were both attended to with a small diamond riffler **(13-23)**.

Set of Towel Bars Project

13-22 A mini die grinder can be used to vein leaves.

13-24 Rounding the underside of the bar.

13-23 Irregularities in the veins can be straightened with a diamond riffler.

13-25 A hole is drilled for clamping the work as well as final mounting.

CARVING THE BAR

Until now, I had been doing all of my experimenting on the small units, and they stood in various stages of development. (If you're going to mess up a part of a project, mess up the one that takes the least amount of material to replace.) All along, I was having trouble clamping and holding them. The top of the bar was still flat, so I clamped the bar to the bench upside down and rounded off the underside and blended it into the twist (13-24).

I suppose that as I worked my subconscious solved the clamping challenge. I drilled a ½-inch hole in the twist to within ½ inch of the bottom (13-25).

Then I continued drilling with a ³⁄₃₂-inch bit to allow me to screw the unit to a scrap with drywall screws. The scrap I then clamped to the bench, and I continued working on the top of the bar and other unfinished aspects of each unit (13-26). The hole will also be used for finally mounting to the wall. The ½-inch hole will be plugged with a dowel.

By now I had the sequence of events down and proceeded to finish the remaining longer units. I started by drilling each and roughing the twist below the bar. The longer units were much easier to work with in that I could clamp them easier and round the bar with a spokeshave (13-27). Marks left by the spoke-

13-26 The work is mounted to a scrap for final work.

13-28 A scraper is used for final smoothing.

13-27 The longer bars are rounded with a spokeshave.

13-29 A gouge is used to round places that the spokeshave couldn't reach.

shave were easily removed with a scraper that I brewed for the occasion **(13–28)**.

Of course, the spokeshave would not reach into the tight spots near the ends of the bar. I used a gouge here for the rounding **(13–29)**. You'll note that I'm again using the mounting holes to fasten the unit to a board clamped to my bench. After turning the unit over and screwing it down again, I could finish up the final detail of the bar **(13–30)**. After that, I cleared my bench of carving tools.

The only thing that remained was sanding the edges of the leaf. You might think that

13-30 The unit is again held with screws for final finishing.

some sort of power device would work well here, perhaps a small drum sander. I've tried them all, and that's why I use a wedge-shaped stick with sandpaper glued to it for all of the convex surfaces (13-31). For the concave surfaces you will note the rounded stick beneath the leaf and to the right in 13-30.

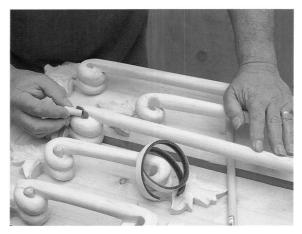

13-32 Foam tape is used to hold the plugs in position.

13-31 Sticks covered with sandpaper are used for final finishing.

PREPARING THE PLUGS

The plugs were all that remained of the project. I cut these from a ½-inch dowel. After shaping a dome on the dowel, I cut off a plug that was about ¼ inch shorter than it should have been. I had no idea what sort of screw the installer would use to mount the units with. I then mounted a short length of foam insulating tape in the bottom of each plug (13-32). This would make the plug fit quite snugly and it could be pushed to an attractive depth without interference from the mounting screw.

I did manage to get a shot of the towel bars in the paint shop (13-33). And the client was kind enough to send me some photos taken in the home (13-34). Sure wish they'd stood a little closer or perhaps hung a towel through them.

13-33 Towel bars in the paint shop.

13-34 (Above and left) Photos of two of the finished products, taken by the client.

Architectural Carving: Techniques for Power & Hand Tools

SPIRAL SHELF SUPPORTS PROJECT

I must say right up front that I'm not responsible for the design of this project and I have no idea where the finished product will wind up. I was commissioned by an architect to carve four pierced spirals $5\frac{1}{2} \times 5$ and 22 inches long. In his original design, the spiral was to make one full turn. I felt obliged to ask what the finished product was to be used for. Pierced spirals can be structurally unsound.

Many years ago a local furniture store had a big promotion, giving away an oak plant stand with each major purchase. This plant stand—about 36 inches tall—had a pierced-spiral pedestal about 4 inches in diameter that made about five turns from base to top. The stand was very attractive, and it would support a plant. If it fell over, however, it would break, as there was little cross-grain strength in the members of the spiral. We repaired those blankety-blank plant stands for years afterward. I remember one older lady that would come through the door of the shop about once a month with the pieces of her plant stand. She always had the same line: "Well, the grandkids were by to visit me again."

When I found out that my spirals were going to support a 3-inch-thick shelf holding examples of Native American pottery, I insisted on a design change. I would carve these supports but only if the spirals made only one-half turn, providing some structural integrity. The modification accepted, I went to work.

LAYOUT & PRELIMINARY STEPS

After turning the blank, I laid out the spiral with a piece of heavy paper from the center of one side to the center of the adjacent side. Then I marked out spots along the line—about 1⅜ inch apart—at which to bore holes. I supported the blank on the drill press in V blocks and was prepared to bore the holes when I came to the startling realization that my drill press had only a 3-inch quill travel and would not bore clear through.

Undaunted, I bored a 3/32-inch hole as deep as I could on the drill press and then used a hand drill to bore the rest of the way through. This hole was to be an accurate guide for the boring to follow. Then I took the stock back to the drill press and bored a series of 1½-inch holes from both sides **(14-1)**.

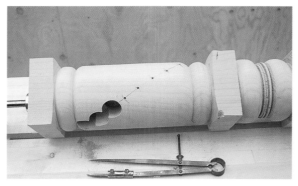

14-1 Layout of the work with some of the larger holes bored.

After marking a centerline and lines 1¼ inch to each side of it, I went to work removing waste **(14-2)**. My object here was to produce a twisted 2½-inch square. The cuts from the lines are made perpendicular to the tangent of the centerline **(14-3)**. That is, they are not made from the lines toward the axis of the round.

I then marked out some centerlines on the square and began to round it off **(14-4)**. The object here was to form a round that flowed into the base and top. In places that were difficult to reach with the air chisel, I resorted to a wide skew **(14-5)**.

I did work with care, but with all of the grain changes, things were still quite ragged. I resorted to a rasp and things then began to flow much better **(14-6)**. The coarse rasp did make things flow but left all surfaces quite rough. To remove the marks of the rasp I resorted to a spokeshave **(14-7)**. In places the spokeshave wouldn't reach I used the fine side of a horseshoe rasp and coarse machinist flies. After that, a few passes with 120-grit sandpaper finished the smoothing.

The only place I had difficulty smoothing was the very base of the piece. My bit had made a rather ragged cut. Not wanting to do all of the sanding necessary to remove marks, I "plastered" the bottom with nitrocellulose

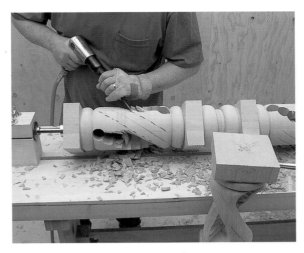

14-2 Preliminary waste removal.

14-3 Cuts are made perpendicular to the tangent of the centerline.

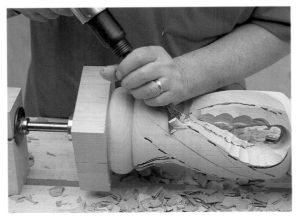

14-4 Rounding off the square.

14-5 A wide skew is used in tight spots.

14-6 A rasp is used for final shaping.

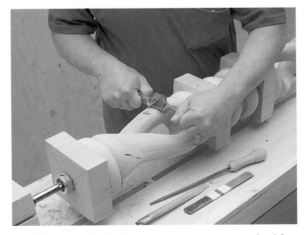

14-7 Tool marks left by the rasp are removed with a spokeshave.

Spiral Shelf Supports Project

patch and sanded it smooth **(14-8)**. Normally I glue sandpaper to a dowel for a task like that, but having no dowel that day, I pressed a piece of plastic pipe into service.

Well, there they are, ready for shipment to some client known only to the architect **(14-9)**. As I look at them I have visions of some carpenter using 20D nails to fasten them in place.

14-8 Tear outs from the drill are patched and sanded.

14-9 The project ready for shipment.

148

PAIR OF CARVED PANELS PROJECT

This pair of panels was designed to go beneath two stained-glass entry lights. The client wanted something similar to the design of the stained glass or at least something with the same flow of lines.

The entry door was particularly ugly, to my eye, and while it couldn't be easily fixed, it could be replaced. Its aesthetic qualities had something to do with the previous owner and burglars. I got to help remedy the situation with the project described in Chapter 17.

DEVELOPING THE PATTERN

After photographing the window I projected the negative onto a piece of paper the exact size of the panel and outlined the foliage. I could see no way of depicting the flowers of the window in wood, so the next step was to develop my own. I couldn't find a lily at the craft store but I did find quite a few photos on the Internet. From these I got an idea of what a lily should look like. It seems that the flower has six petals, three large and three small.

I started by rolling out some clay between two ¼-inch sticks to keep the thickness consistent (15-1). I did a rough sketch of a circle that I determined to be the size of the flower, and then I sketched one petal on the clay (15-2).

After cutting it out, I used it as a pattern to cut two more of this larger petal. Then I cut out the three smaller petals in the same manner. After shaping each petal, I assembled a flower on a clean sheet of paper (15-3). Once I got it looking like I thought it should, I drew it on the paper, doing a little careful sighting (15-4).

So that I wouldn't have two flowers that looked exactly the same, I tipped the model and outlined the tipped version (15-5). At this point I wasn't quite sure I could depict a tipped flower on the panel, but at least I had two different flowers.

Looking at the pattern, I noticed that all of the leaves were flat. As long as I had tipping on the brain, I cut a couple of leaves from the clay, twisted them, and added them to the pattern (15-6).

When I transferred the pattern to the blank, I used a colored pencil so that I could be sure I traced all of the lines (15-7).

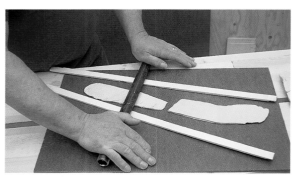

15-1 Clay is prepared by rolling it out between sticks that hold the thickness constant.

15-3 Clay petals are assembled on a sheet of paper.

15-2 One petal is sketched on the clay.

15-4 The flower is sketched using the clay model as a guide.

Architectural Carving: Techniques for Power & Hand Tools

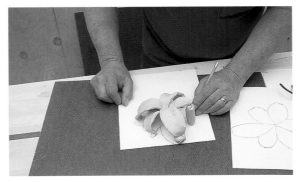

15-5 The model is tipped for a second view.

15-6 A clay model is used to depict twisted leaves.

15-7 A colored pencil is used to transfer the pattern.

SETTING IN THE DESIGN

After I transferred the pattern to the blank, I began vigorously to attack it with my router. Big macho me, I managed to cut away a portion that should have been left—see **15-8**, at the tip of the pencil. I did not cry. I did strike my breast three times while saying, "Mea culpa," and shaded all of the areas that *should* be removed with a pencil to avoid further errors.

Actually I had taken the panel outdoors to do the routing—a great deal of dust developed and I feared it would reach the pilot light of the gas furnace, blowing the roof off of the shop and me into the next county. It was 16 degrees F (−9 degrees C) that morning and I wasn't paying as much attention to my work as I should have—more attention given to my frozen fingertips and ears.

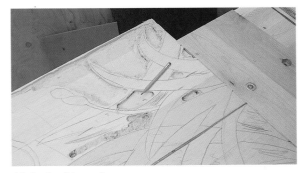

15-8 Accidents happen.

PATCHING

Once the panel was routed, the first thing to receive attention was the area I cut out by mistake. After cleaning up the edges of the area, I made a paper pattern of the area that needed a patch. This I did by placing a piece of paper over the area and rubbing it with a pencil **(15-9)**. After transferring the pattern to a piece of $7/16$-inch basswood, I cut it out and glued it in place.

15-9 Preparing a pattern for a patch.

Pair of Carved Panels Project

151

CLEANING UP WHAT THE ROUTER LEFT

Normally I don't rout right up to the lines. Rather, I leave the line plus about $\frac{1}{16}$ inch. In delicate cross-grain areas I leave even more. I can "sneak up on" these areas later, making a number of careful cuts **(15–10)**. The router can tear out these delicate areas very easily. This particular panel is not very precise at all—as I mentioned, it was very chilly that morning and I wanted to get back into the warm as fast as I could.

There are a number of ways of removing what the router didn't. You can use mallet and gouge or chisel **(15–11)**. This, of course, will work, but you are likely to leave marks from the overlapping of the gouge cuts that will need to be cleaned up later. In delicate areas, you are likely to chip away wanted material. And, there is a tendency to overcut below the ground. In all of this cleanup work I tend to make all cuts slightly above the ground. I just might want to change the design slightly as I work and I don't want any overcuts to contend with.

My favorite tool for this work is a large skew. It works particularly well on outside curves. I usually "sneak up on" the line with several cuts, and I can feel if the cut is true and flowing. Waste is usually chipped away from the ground, making a grounding cut unnecessary. The skew can also be used on gentle inside curves and sometimes even for cutting against the grain **(15–12)**.

I have made some pencil lines in **15–12** to indicate grain direction, and yes, I am cutting against the *surface grain,* but note, the blade is cutting from the top the ground and essentially *with* the grain.

Sometimes I walk the skew down the line—that is, placing the heel of the skew firmly on the line, then lifting the handle while guiding the blade along the line. This

15-10 Plenty of "meat" is left near fragile areas.

15-11 Removing waste with mallet and gouge.

15-12 A skew can be used on gentle inside curves.

walking technique works especially well on tighter-radius inside curves, but here, rather than walking a skew, I walk a gouge that has a sweep a little tighter than the curve **(15–13)**.

Architectural Carving: Techniques for Power & Hand Tools

15-13 A gouge is "walked" around inside curves.

WORKING THE STEMS

The stems presented a little challenge. I left plenty of "meat" in the stem area since it was not well defined on the pattern and I wanted them to be of proper and consistent width. First, I carefully trued one side, making sure that it flowed with no bumps. Next, I used a pair of dividers to mark the other side, letting one leg of the dividers ride the trued side and the other cut into the wood (15-14). I used one setting for the dividers as they scribed from the crotch to the foliage, then a smaller setting from the crotch to the flower. The stems that go to the buds are even smaller.

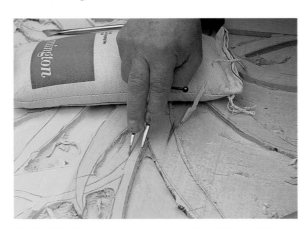

15-14 Dividers are used to keep the sides of the stems parallel.

Oh, that green and white bag resting on the work in 15-14? That's a bag of lead shot, placed there to hold the patches in place until the glue dries. Fortunately, it is large enough to cover all three. Did I say "patches?" Did I say, "three?" I don't want to talk about it.

USING DIVIDERS

The dividers I'm using are a small, inexpensive pair that have been bored to receive scribing needles. I keep the needles very sharp, and they will actually do some cutting. Your dividers don't need scribing needles, but sharpen the points with a fine file—and keep them moving against the grain. That way they won't tend to follow the grain and distort the mark.

Taking a break from the cleanup work, I decided to determine just how the foliage would lie, which leaf overlapped which. I drew a red line down any leaf—or portion of leaf—that would be on top (15-15). I drew black squiggles on leaf portions that would be low. And since I intended to tip some of the leaves, I put a few green lines in areas that would be tipped.

15-15 Different colors are used to note the relief of various components.

Pair of Carved Panels Project

153

As I was drawing the colored lines, I noticed that some of the leaf outlines were quite ragged. That is somewhat to be expected considering that I drew the pattern over rough exterior plywood. Then there was the error in transfer, etc. No problem. I bent a flexible straightedge over the average of these lines and drew a true and darker line (15–16).

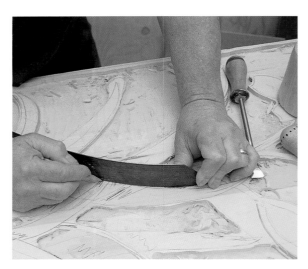

154

15-16 A flexible straightedge is used to true irregular lines.

15-17 Waste is removed from tight spots with a V tool.

CLEANUP WORK

The object or this cleanup work is exactly that, cleanup. It's not necessary to produce totally finished edges at this time. It has always been my failing as a carver to do too much detail work too soon. Things often change as the work progresses—many times have I found myself cutting away some area on which I spent a good deal of time and effort.

During the cleanup work I never cut any edge completely to the ground, leaving as much as $\frac{1}{32}$ inch of material untouched. As I said, things can change, and if any areas are overcut into the ground, as changes are made these cuts will show in the finished product.

There were plenty of tight spots that the router couldn't reach even had I wanted it to. I cut into these with a V tool (15–17), removing as much waste as I could, leaving anything I couldn't get to for later.

WORKING THE LEAVES

The first order of business in working the leaves is to establish the plane of the face of each leaf. Leaves turn and twist and it wouldn't look right if all of the faces of the leaves were parallel to the ground. I used a large skew to alter the plane of each leaf (15–18), using the green lines I made earlier to show me which leaf turned in which direction. A glance at the pencil resting on a leaf face in 15–18 will give you an idea as to how much I tipped some leaves.

Cutting the raised vein of the leaf was a simple, three-step process. First, with a tight-sweep gouge, I cut down each side of a centerline I had drawn on the leaf (15–19). Next, I used a wider-sweep gouge—the side toward the outer edge of the leaf cutting, the inner side riding on the vein (15–20). I followed

15-18 A large skew is used to establish the plane of each leaf.

15-20 A wider-sweep gouge is used to blend the vein into the leaf.

15-19 A tight-sweep gouge is used to expose the leaf vein.

15-21 A yet wider-sweep gouge is used for further blending.

with a yet wider-sweep gouge used in the same manner **(15-21)**.

Some portions tipped quite severely, and this would affect the position of the vein. To make sure I had the vein in the correct position, I made another model. After cutting a leaf in clay, I shaped it with a gouge to represent a vein **(15-22)**. I could then twist this model to any desired shape to aid me in carving **(15-23)**.

One leaf was straight and not very interesting at all. I decided to twist it all the way around. Here again the model came in handy for drawing the new leaf as well as serving as a guide for carving **(15-24)**.

15-22 A gouge can be used to shape clay models.

Pair of Carved Panels Project

15-23 A twisted model is used to aid carving.

15-25 Drilling a small hole at the center of the flower with a small gouge.

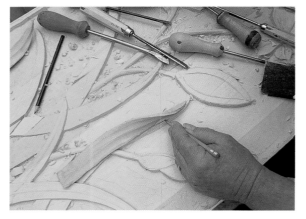

15-24 A completely twisted model is used for another effect.

15-26 The petals are parted with a V tool.

WORKING THE FLOWERS & BUDS

The first step in working the flowers was to make a parting cut in the center. This amounted to drilling a hole with a small gouge **(15-25)**. As work progressed I deepened it to a point where the bottom lay about $3/16$ inch below the ground. Next, I parted the petals with a V tool **(15-26)** and established the plane of each petal with a shallow-sweep gouge **(15-27)**. The plane of the petals dives quickly for the ground at the tip and also in the center while leaving a gentler curve at the center. Also, each petal is cupped substantially. I was careful to leave some extra "meat" on the larger petals at the center, for over these areas stood the plant's reproductive parts. These I parted with a V tool **(15-28)**. It was then a matter of putting in the raised vein of each petal **(15-29)**, and I'm here to say that carving that vein and avoiding the delicate stamen was not easy.

One petal on one flower made a complete twist to the point where the back of the petal could be seen. You can be certain I had a model handy **(15-30)** to make sure I got it right.

Final smoothing of the petal was done with sandpaper. Any areas that the sandpaper would not easily reach felt the pass of a riffler **(15-31)**.

Architectural Carving: Techniques for Power & Hand Tools

15-27 The plane of the petals is established with a shallow gouge.

15-29 Veins are added to each petal.

15-30 A model is used in carving a twisted petal.

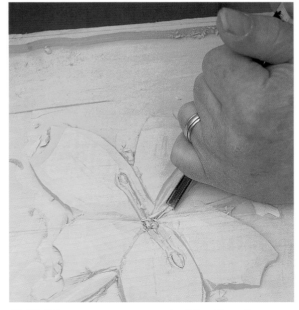

15-28 The stamens are parted with a V tool.

15-31 Rifflers are used to smooth tight spots.

157

Pair of Carved Panels Project

After the flowers, the buds were a very simple matter. First I made some parting cuts with a V tool, then I rounded off all surfaces with a skew **(15-32)**.

To this point I had only been playing with rounding off the stems. Now I got serious and dropped the points where they entered the flower and rounded the edges **(15-33)**. I started with a small chisel, but found that in some areas a back-bent gouge worked very well and left a much more evenly rounded stem **(15-34)**.

15-34 A back-bent gouge works well for rounding the stems.

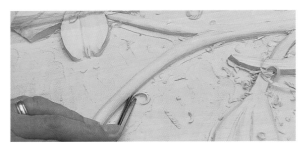

15-35 The V tool is used to undercut the stems slightly.

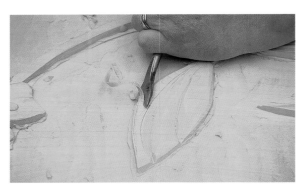

15-32 A skew is used to shape the surface of the buds.

15-36 For texturing, a shallow gouge is used to make random-length cuts.

15-33 The stems are dropped to proper plane and rounded.

To give the stems an even more rounded appearance, I undercut them with a V tool **(15-35)**. I even did this around some of the leaves and petals.

At this point, I breathed a sigh of relief that the hard work was done and only the repetitious and time-consuming operation of texturing the ground remained.

TEXTURING THE GROUND

For a light texture, I chose a shallow gouge, making random-length cuts to an equal depth **(15-36)**. You will note the pencil lines on the ground. It is often difficult to see when the ground is completely textured. It's very easy to miss spots that will show in the finished product. Once all of the pencil lines are removed, you can rest assured that you didn't miss anything significant.

Throughout the panel the standing characters were not outlined to the total depth of the

Architectural Carving: Techniques for Power & Hand Tools

ground, so that alterations could be made in their shape as might be required. Now was the time to cut them completely to the ground and, in most cases, overcut them slightly. I found a knife well suited to the operation **(15–37)**. In areas that I had undercut—especially along the stems—I was careful to get the knife's point into the bottom of the V-tool cut.

15-37 **A knife is used for final parting cuts.**

In most cases, I cut toward the characters. In some tight spots it was necessary to rock the tool back and forth to make sure that the waste was cut free and not torn.

In some areas I found that I was cutting against the grain and the gouge would start to dig in. I immediately stopped pushing and let the waste stand to mark the area, then I came back and cut from the other side **(15–38)**.

Also, because of the grain, I had to cut away from some characters. This left a small area with no texture. To texture these areas, I used a scraper with the same curve as the gouge **(15–39)**.

15-38 **A chip is left standing to warn of grain direction.**

The panels received a "painted" finish. If you have read the chapter on finishing you'll probably note that they were used for the demonstration on strikeout and glaze.

I delivered the panels to be installed by a carpenter who was doing other work in the home. Two days later I got a frantic call from the lady of the house. It seems that the carpenter couldn't figure out how to fit the bottom piece of stop because of the design. He wanted to cut off the panel and set it on top of the stop. I cringed, then sped to the home. I take offense when someone wants to cut one of my panels. The nice young carpenter was quite attentive as I attacked that bottom piece of stop with nothing more than a pair of dividers, coping saw, and a pocketknife.

All in all, I thought the finished product was quite attractive **(15–40)**. Of course, my thoughts don't count. The homeowner was satisfied and that's what counts.

15-39 **A scraper is used to texture tight spots.**

15-40 **One of the finished panels.**

Pair of Carved Panels Project

16

PAIR OF COLUMN CAPITALS PROJECT

I like columns. They give me a chance to do some heavy work and get good exercise, and the work's a little unusual. This pair of columns is not going to support anything. The column itself will actually slide into the capital rather than support it. The reason for this being: the columns sit on a concrete pad. Frost could cause the pad to rise. This would tear the overhead structure from the building.

The clients wanted something a bit original. They wanted a classical look but not a classical copy. For instance, they wanted all four sides of the capitals to be identical. This is not a classical approach. But the clients were a pleasure to work for, and there was no designer involved.

The lady of the house did not like the volute in the pictures I was showing them. She said that it had too many turns and made her dizzy. The man of the house said that the pictures were too frilly as he pointed to the egg-and-dart mold at the base of the capital. He said, "Could we just round this over and not put the design in it?" I was beginning to smile. This commission was going to be a snap, a quick volute and no egg-and-dart.

Departing further from the traditional they wanted beads cut on each side of the flat portion of the volute. I'd never done this before and had no idea just how it would work, but some you win and some you lose.

INITIAL WORK

The first step is to do a little drawing. Here I like roofing felt. I can make lines on it with scribing devices for accuracy. I can also cut various pieces from it as patterns. As the lines don't show up in photos well, I have drawn over the scribed lines with colored pencil for your benefit (16-1).

The inner circle represents the column. The outer circle represents the limit of what was to be the mold I intended to carve in the capital. Other lines represent the extremities of the volutes at each corner. On the piece of felt to the right is a rough sketch of the volutes.

Now, this project would have been simpler if the lumber dealer had some 16/4 stock, but he didn't. With the client dancing from one foot to another, I opted to use 8/4 stock rather than wait for a new shipment of 16/4. This, of course, entailed a lot of pieces,

16-1 Felt paper is sketched for a pattern.

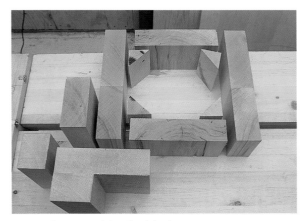

16-2 Pieces used in the blank.

161

and I have set them out on the bench unassembled (16-2).

I did cut the wider pieces from a long glue-up (16-3, left). That glue-up was about four feet long when I started. I also tried to do any preassembling in length (16-3, right).

I did try to glue the pieces as carefully and accurately as possible, for guess who was going to smooth out any irregularities for the next round of gluing (16-4)? After using that hand plane, I ran some 80-grit sandpaper glued to a flat block to smooth out the irregularities of the plane. A good, tightly fitting glue joint is essential here. And yes, as these are going to be exterior fixtures, I used moisture-resistant yellow glue.

Pair of Column Capitals Project

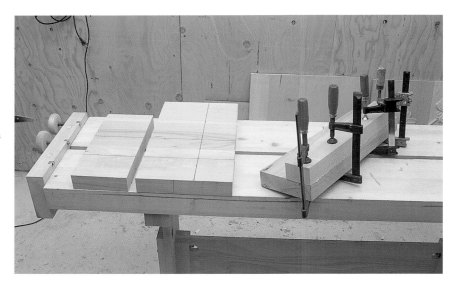

16-3 Work is done with large pieces at first.

162

16-4 Truing irregularities with a hand plane.

WORKING WITH THE PATTERNS

While the glue was drying I went back to the pattern. After cutting out the pattern and trying it on the blank, I found that it was not quite what I wanted. I taped the cut-out piece back in and tried again (16-5). Then I was able to mark the blank. Note that I've cut only one quadrant of the pattern. The remaining portion left in the square helps me keep the pattern located.

16-5 If an error is made in cutting the felt, it can be taped back in place and cut again.

Architectural Carving: Techniques for Power & Hand Tools

The volute I drew on a piece of printer paper as large as I could and then reduced it with a copy machine. I outlined this on the blank using transfer paper **(16-6)**.

16-6 The volute is outlined using transfer paper.

SETTING IN THE VOLUTE & SHAPING THE BLANK

I began the setting-in process by pushing a gouge that matched the curve around the lines **(16-7)**. As the radius of the curve changes continually, it's almost impossible to find enough gouges to match it exactly. I usually use a gouge with a sweep slightly greater than the curve. It took me only four different gouges to set in this volute.

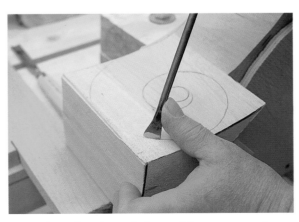

16-7 The volute is set in by pushing a gouge along the lines.

The next step was to remove waste along the set line **(16-8)**. As I was removing waste around the center of the volute **(16-9)**, I could see that I was doing a lot of precision work for nothing—not very efficient. I drew some lines down ½ inch from the surface of the blank and began with vigor to set in only the center of the volute **(16-10)**. You'll note in **16-10** that I have clamped a stick to the bench to support the blank. The drag on the shaft of my contrived vise was not quite sufficient to keep the blank from rotating.

16-8 Waste is removed along the set lines.

16-9 Removing waste around the center of the volute.

163

16-10 Only the center of the volute is set in.

Ah, but now how to transfer the pattern with the center of the volute standing? Easy—cut a hole for it in both pattern and transfer paper **(16-11)**.

16-11 A hole is cut in the center of the pattern to make transfer possible.

With the pattern once again transferred, I went to work shaping the outer edge **(16-12)**. Why the clamps? You can see that I added the little block marked X to the blank. As I worked I could see that that was not going to be enough to accept the whole inner portion of the volute. After mumbling a few choice names for my lumber dealer and his lack of 12/4 material, I added the two pieces marked O.

16-12 Shaping the outer edge.

The shaping of the edge was simple until I reached the inside. Here I could only cut across the grain and slightly with it **(16-13)**. That little knot toward the center was sure to tear out, but it posed no challenge for my little disk grinder and some 16-grit sandpaper **(16-14)**.

16-13 Cutting a tight spot in the outer edge.

The next step was to sketch in the depth of the remaining portion of the volute **(16-15)**, after which I set in and smoothed it out carefully. I further smoothed both face and outer edge with a rasp **(16-16)**. I wanted all of the surfaces to be smooth and flowing, for this first volute was to be used to derive a pattern from which to mark all of the others **(16-17)**.

16-16 All surfaces are smoothed with a rasp.

16-14 A disk grinder can be used to cut knots.

16-17 The first finished volute is used to derive a pattern for the rest.

16-15 The volute is set in.

As I continued marking with the paper pattern, the center hole became quite ragged, and that ragged line became increasingly hard to follow with a gouge. After using the pattern to mark the "average" of the center character and to locate it, I used a drawing template to draw a nice neat circle **(16-18)**.

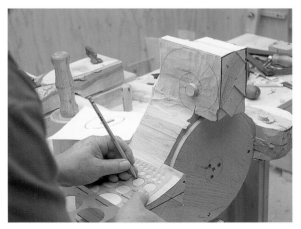

16-18 A drawing template is used in lieu of the ragged pattern.

Now that I had received some good exercise on the first volute, it was time to get to work in earnest. Out came the air chisel. The first step was to chamfer the edge to the depth line so that I could see the location from the opposite side of the blank. Then I found that, if I was careful, I could remove most of the waste down to the depth line **(16-19)**.

16-19 **Most of the waste is removed with an air chisel.**

Once I had a reasonably flat surface around the center character, I marked out the whole volute and set it in. The air chisel came in very handy for removing that large amount of waste near the front, though I did have to be aware of the grain change at the center **(16-20)**.

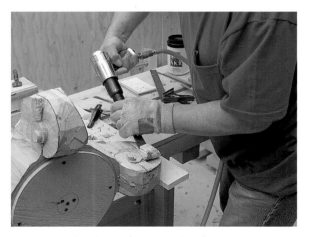

16-20 **Caution is used near grain changes.**

Once I set the air chisel aside, I finished up smoothing with a shallow gouge, cutting from the outer edge toward the center **(16-21)**.

After doing some sketching to get an idea about how the rest of the capital characters would look, I set in the rest of the periphery of the volute. Toward the center of the capital there was one little area that defied good, clean parting cuts. Deep areas that run with the grain are my nemesis. I should say that they were my nemesis until I discovered the mini die grinder and a straight carbide cutter **(16-22)**.

16-21 **A shallow gouge is used for finishing the volute.**

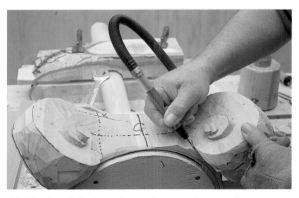

16-22 **A mini die grinder is used for parting cuts with the grain.**

At this point I decided to clean up the outer edge of all of the volutes. I went around each with a rasp, making sure that I had a flowing surface **(16-23)**. I trued only the edge of the surface, leaving the center any way that it hap-

16-23 A rasp is used to make the surfaces flow.

pened to be. I wanted only a mark on the edge. Now, if you will excuse me for a moment, for dust purposes I'm going to remove the shaft from the pillow blocks and take the assembly outdoors and smooth the center portion of the periphery of the volutes with my angle grinder.

With a nice smooth periphery I could now cut in the beads. To mark the beads I did consider a transfer-paper pattern but dismissed the idea. Rather I cut some decreasing widths of clay for the purpose (16-24). The clay was a bit difficult to control along the outer edge so I made a dotted line, supporting the clay with my finger. Later I came back and filled in between the dots using the old reliable "finger scribe"—that is, holding the pen in thumb and forefinger while letting the middle finger ride the edge (16-25).

I then went around the design with a V tool, just barely leaving the lines (16-26). Noting that the center character in its present state would interfere with the work that was to follow, I rounded it off (16-27).

16-25 One finger rides the edge as the pen marks.

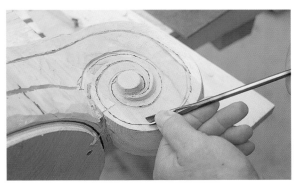

16-26 A V tool is used to begin setting in the beads.

16-24 A clay model with a decreasing width is used to mark the beads.

16-27 The center character is rounded off.

167

Pair of Column Capitals Project

Now with mallet and gouge I made stop cuts for setting in the beads **(16–28)**. To remove waste between the stop cuts I used a shallow gouge, cutting toward the bead **(16–29)**, then followed up with a shallow gouge for final smoothing **(16–30)**. It did take several widths of shallow gouge to complete the process **(16–31)**. When my narrowest gouge was too wide, I resorted to a riffler **(16–32)**.

I chose a small chisel to round off the outer edges of the beads **(16–33)**. For the inner edges I resorted to a tiny V tool **(16–34)**. A few passes with some stiff sandpaper finished the bead operation **(16–35)**.

16-29 A shallow gouge is used to remove waste between the beads.

16-28 Mallet and gouge are used to set in the beads.

16-30 A shallow gouge is used for final smoothing.

16-31 A very small gouge is used to complete the process.

Architectural Carving: Techniques for Power & Hand Tools

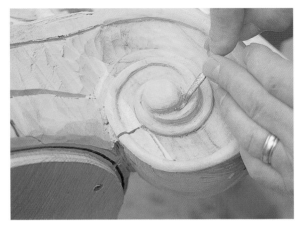

16-32 A riffler is used in the tightest of spots.

16-33 A small chisel is used to round off the beads.

16-34 A tiny V tool is used on the inner edges.

169

16-35 Stiff sandpaper finishes the beads.

SOME THOUGHTS ON CUTTING BEADS

I did learn a couple of things on that first set of beads. The first being, that my somewhat shaky lines were somewhat distracting. After setting in the beads, I sanded off the lines to evaluate the rough bead and make sure that I had made flowing cuts **(16-36)**.

The second thing that I learned was that there was a very fragile area toward the center of the capital. I split out the first while using mallet and gouge and had to glue it back in. On the rest of the volutes, I made my parting cut with a knife **(16-37)**.

At this point I removed the waste between the beads in the center portion of the capital and rounded off the lower, center bead **(16-38)**.

While I worked on this final stage, I thought of the exterior latex paint that was most likely to be used on these capitals and how it would fill anything that was not well defined. To finish things off, I went back and made a stop cut around the inner edge of the bead and deepened the relief with a gouge **(16-39)**.

16-36 Lines are removed with sandpaper and the bead is evaluated.

16-38 Waste is removed and the beads are rounded off.

16-37 To prevent splitting, a knife is used to make parting cuts.

16-39 Beads are deepened with a gouge.

170

DOOR WITH CARVED PANELS PROJECT

17

As an architectural carver, you will be called upon to embellish sash of various types. These clients had been searching for carved doors but found nothing that was to their liking. In addition the jamb was an odd size and any new door would have to be fit to it. Cutting down any manufactured door would leave it a bit strange looking, and there was the problem of getting the lock and passage set to fit the reduced styles. Enter the custom builder.

The commission for this exterior door followed the pair of carved floral panels that went below the stained-glass lights, as described in Chapter 15.

PREPARING THE SASH

For years, I was under the opinion that the only "proper" way to join the members of any door was with a mortise-and-tenon joint. That was until I was called upon to repair an old door that was doweled together. This particular door had been water damaged but only to the extent that the hide glue joints had fallen apart. After cleaning the joints and reassembling the door, I found it every bit as stout as a door that had been joined with mortise-and-tenon joints.

This experience changed my opinion of doweled doors. Now, were I to make several doors, I would use a mortise-and-tenon system. It goes more quickly; but to set up the machinery for a single door is time consuming, especially setting up the cope head on the tenoning machine to fit the knives of the sticker that runs the sash mold. For a single door, I resort to dowels, and I can use any sash mold I want. It will be mitered, and there is no worry that I have a matching cope cutter.

The first and most important step in any sash work is to carefully face and straighten one edge of the slightly oversize members of the sash on a good jointer. You can't expect any sash to be flat if its individual components are twisted or warped.

After the members are planed to thickness, they should be cut to width and length. I usually cut the stiles to ½ inch over the desired length. This leaves me a little to trim in the case of an out-of-square jamb, and leaves a little to scribe to the threshold. The rails should all be cut long by twice the width of the sash mold. The reason will become obvious as we move on. This door has one mullion that I leave long, to be fit later.

After laying out the location of the rails on the stiles, I set each rail in place and mark the location of the dowels **(17-1)**. I mark these at random, being concerned only that they don't interfere with the rabbet or an area at the bottom that will likely be trimmed in hanging. This randomness ensures that I will get the members in the proper location during assembly.

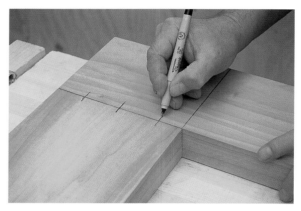

17-1 Rails are set in place in order to mark the location of the dowels.

It would be wonderful to have a horizontal-boring machine for drilling the dowel holes, but I don't have such a machine. I resort to a doweling jig. I really don't even have a proper doweling jig. I prepare one from a piece of 8/4 scrap by squaring it up and drilling a hole in it on my drill press. A piece of plywood fastened to it gives me something to clamp to the various members—and, a hole in the ply allows me to locate the lines indicating the position of the dowels **(17-2)**. When using any type of doweling jig, remember that it is a guide for the bit. It's not intended to force the bit into the proper angle and location. Use a gentle touch.

A doweling jig is not the most accurate way to bore holes, but the dowels that I will be using are a few thousandths of an inch undersized. A little inaccuracy will actually be a blessing, forcing each dowel to one side or the other of the bores.

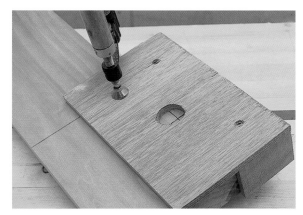

17-2 A shop-made doweling jig.

Once all of the holes are bored, the next step is cutting the sash mold and the rabbet. For the sash mold I used a router. I cut the rabbet with two passes over the table saw **(17-3)**. I intended to stop all panels in from the back. The upper panel with lights would have to be removable in case of damage to the lights. The lower panels could have been set in a dado, but I got conned into installing this door, and anything that would make it lighter and easier to handle seemed a blessing. I intended to fit the sash before installing any panels.

17-3
Two passes through a table saw are needed to cut the rabbet.

After mold and rabbet are cut, I deepen the dowel holes to accommodate a 3½-inch dowel **(17-4)**. My doweling jig would not permit me to drill the holes to the full depth required.

After inserting a couple of dowels into each rail, I marked each extremity of the sash mold using a scrap to extend its location **(17-5)**.

CUTTING THE RABBET & RAILS

Note that the first character of the sash mold is a small flat area perpendicular to the face of the member. The rabbet should be cut to exactly that depth and the rails should be cut long by twice that amount.

17-4 Dowel holes are deepened to receive a 3½-inch dowel.

17-5 The extremities of the sash mold are marked using a scrap to extend their location.

173

Door With Carved Panels Project

Using a scrap cut at a 45-degree angle and clamped in the rabbet as a guide, I cut the miters in the stile sash mold (17-6). (The miters on the rails were cut earlier on a table saw.) This should be done very carefully, paying attention to which side of the line to cut on. I prefer the cuts be a little long, if anything. They can be trimmed to fit later on.

Waste removal was handled with a chisel (17-7). For final waste removal, I used a shallow gouge, slightly hollowing the area beneath the waste (17-8). Not being the trusting kind, I then set the rail in place and checked to see that it set squarely with the stile (17-9). It didn't.

17-6 Miters are cut using a scrap cut at a 45-degree angle as a guide.

17-7 Waste is removed with a chisel.

17-8 The area beneath the rail is hollowed slightly with a shallow gouge.

17-9 The rail is set in place and checked for square.

Architectural Carving: Techniques for Power & Hand Tools

The error was not great, and a couple of passes with a scraper over the front edge of the stile corrected it **(17-10)**. If the error had been greater, I would have used a dogleg chisel to remove considerably more material **(17-11)**. The dogleg works much like a small plane—and, if the error had been less, I would have used a block coated with coarse sandpaper **(17-12)**. The block also works well for cleaning up any irregularities left by the dogleg chisel.

17-10 A scraper can be used to adjust the stile socket.

17-11 If the error is great, a dogleg chisel is in order.

17-12 For a slight error, a sandpaper-coated block can be used.

Door With Carved Panels Project

Any irregularity in the miter cut can be corrected with a chisel **(17-13)**. If the miter cut is only slightly oversized, I don't worry about it. Poplar has a good "squash factor." If the miter cut were short, I would apply a little patch to the members during assembly, in much the same way that a bricklayer would use mortar. I, of course, would chastise myself thoroughly and don sackcloth and ashes for the final assembly.

As a final step I assembled the door without glue and fit in the mullion **(17-14)**. To mark the position of the dowel, I used a dowel point **(17-15)**. No great strength is required here. The dowel is only to hold the mullion in place.

All that was left was final assembly. The best type of dowel to use here is a spiral-fluted dowel. Second best would be a straight-fluted dowel. I'm too cheap to buy either. I buy 3-foot lengths of dowel and flute them by dragging the teeth of a saw over them **(17-16)**.

17-13 Errors in the miter cut can be corrected with a chisel.

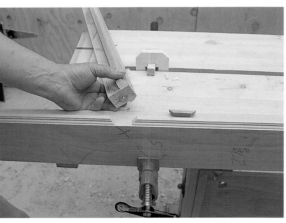

17-15 A dowel point is used to mark the hole's location.

17-14 The door is assembled dry and the mullion fit.

17-16 A dowel can be fluted by dragging it across the teeth of a saw.

176

Architectural Carving: Techniques for Power & Hand Tools

PREPARING THE PANELS

The easiest way to prepare the face of linenfold panels is to have a mill run the stock through their sticker (molding machine). I went to my son's shop and took one look at the sticker, thought about the setup time, thought about the hold-downs I would have to rig for the additional width of these panels, and decided to cut the face with a router.

I began by making a full-scale drawing of both the linenfold design and the end view of the panel, using the router bits I would be using to aid in the drawing **(17-17)**.

After cutting the linenfold pattern out, I transferred the design to the panel **(17-18)**. Waste around the outer edge of the panel was removed with two passes over the table saw, much the same as the rabbet was cut in the door members. To finish up, I cut the end design of the linenfold into the panel **(17-19)**.

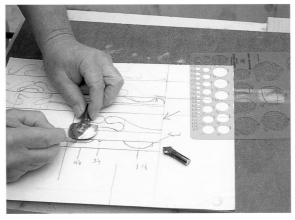

17-17 Router bits intended to cut the design are used to aid in drawing.

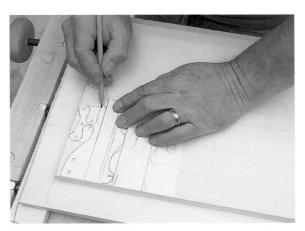

17-18 The linenfold design is transferred to the panel.

17-19 The outline of the linenfold is set into the panel.

Then I cut the end design from the drawing and used it to set the depth of my router bits **(17-20)**. With a scrap of 8/4 material as thick as the panels, and a piece of plywood along with a few clamps, I set up a jig to guide my router **(17-21)**. Rather than trying to cut in one pass, I made several. A mark on the case of the router made it possible to set the correct maximum depth **(17-22)**. A block plane, a cove plane, and some assorted scrapers helped me to make cuts that the router couldn't **(17-23)**. I've placed them on the panel in the location of the cuts they made. In places where nothing would work, I resorted to my trusty dogleg chisel **(17-24)**.

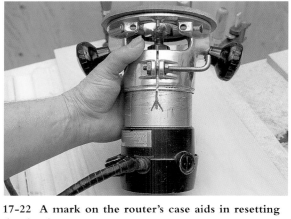

17-22 A mark on the router's case aids in resetting the depth.

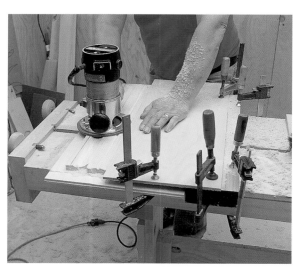

17-20 A paper pattern is used to set the depth of the router bit.

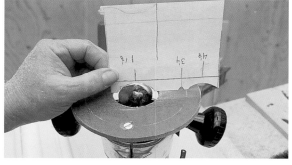

17-23 Assorted hand tools finish off the router cuts.

17-24 When all other tools fail, a dogleg chisel can be used.

17-21 A jig is improvised to guide the router.

178

Architectural Carving: Techniques for Power & Hand Tools

MAKING CUTS THE ROUTER CAN'T MAKE

If you don't happen to have a cove plane, you can improvise by gluing pieces of curved wood to the bottom of a small block plane and grinding the iron to fit the wood. You can also build a cove plane with no more than a block of wood, a bolt, a nut, and a couple of pieces of steel **(17–25)**. Make a ¼-inch dado cut almost through the block at a 45-degree angle **(17–26)**. Drill a large hole near the end of the dado to receive curling chips. Drill another hole perpendicular to the dado to receive a bolt that will hold the iron in place. If you square off the large hole, it will keep the nut on the locking bolt from turning.

I made my iron from a piece of tool steel cut from an old disposable saw blade, but you could purchase an inexpensive block plane and use the iron from it. For the hold-down/chip-curler I used a piece of ⅛-inch-thick steel strap, beveled on the end.

Round off the bottom of the block with a hand plane to the desired cove and grind the iron to fit **(17–27)**. This little contrivance works quite well, although it often clogs with chips. Keep a stick handy to clean out the chips as you think of the money you saved.

17-25 **Components of a shop-built cove plane.**

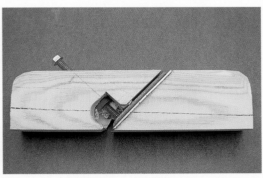

17-26 **A shop-built cove plane assembled.**

17-27 **The iron is ground to fit the block.**

179

Door With Carved Panels Project

With this assortment of tools, I came up with a shaped panel **(17-28)**.

I then cut windows in my pattern and used them to mark the curves on the inside of the linenfold **(17-29)**. With these points located, I could then sketch in the rest of the design.

I then set in the outer portion of the linenfold to the imagined thickness of the linen—about ⅛ inch **(17-30)**. Then I set in and rounded off the inner portions of the design **(17-31)**. Note that I have avoided the areas marked with an X. After beveling the extremes

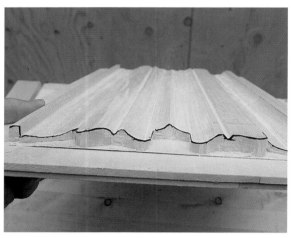

17-28 End view of the shaped panel.

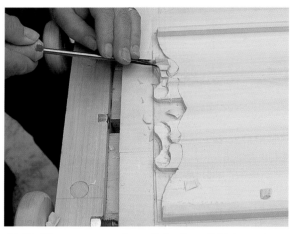

17-30 The outer portion of the linenfold is set in.

17-29 Windows are cut in the pattern for marking.

17-31 The inner portion is set in and rounded off.

of the inner portion to the depth of the set-in **(17-32)**, I made a stop cut along the curve **(17-33)**. This stop cut should be deep, away from the center of the design, and nonexistent at the center. The uncut area represents the edge of the linen. This cut was executed by tilting the gouge so that only one corner dug in. Then, with a gouge, waste was removed to the stop cut **(17-34)**.

The first time I carved a linenfold, I had a terrible time envisioning what I was doing. I made a clay model and even that didn't help much. I finally wound up making a clay model that was gray on one side and red on the other. That got me through the first linenfold.

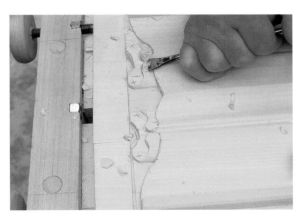

17-32 The extremes are beveled.

17-33 Stop cuts are made along the curve.

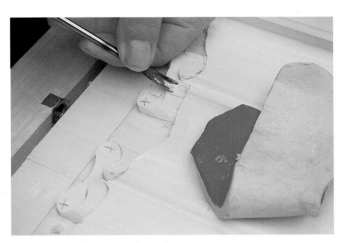

17-34 Waste is removed to the stop cut.

As you progress you might need to deepen the stop cut. Be sure to tip the gouge so that nothing is cut near the center of the design **(17-35)**. The outer portions were carved in the same manner: bevel, stop cut, and waste removal **(17-36)**.

At this point I was ready to clean up the ground but realized that I hadn't finished setting in the whole design. I quickly finished by rounding the extremes of the design **(17-37)**.

After walking tools around the design, I found a skew the best tool for cleaning up the ground **(17-38)**. Any saw marks disappeared quickly beneath a small scraper **(17-39)**.

Yes, I've been putting off that last linen curl. I like to leave the easy parts for last. This last curl also fell to the three steps: bevel to the thickness **(17-40)**, stop cut **(17-41)**, and waste removal **(17-42)**.

182   **17-35 The gouge is tipped to prevent cutting near the center of the curve.**

17-36 Waste is removed to the set cut.

17-37 The extremes of the design are rounded.

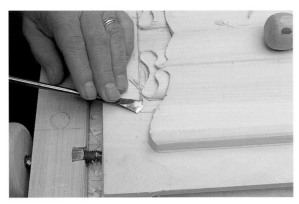

17-38 A skew works well for cleaning up the ground.

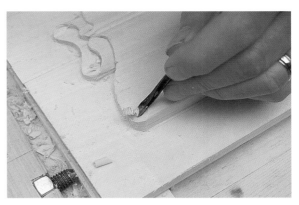

17-40 Bevel.

17-39 A small scraper is used to remove saw marks.

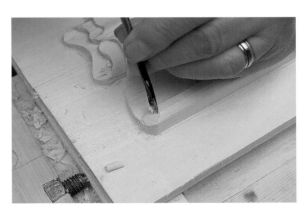

17-41 Stop cut.

17-42 Waste removal.

As a final step, I rounded off the sharp edges slightly **(17-43)**. This will cause them to pick up light to form a contrast with the shadows of the design. Now that the panels are finished **(17-44)**, if you'll excuse me, I'll go fit and hang the sash.

Waiting to install the panels until after the door was fit was one of my better ideas. The sash alone weighed only forty pounds. With the panels and lights installed the door weighed 90 pounds. The upper panel with the lights is composed of two pieces of ¾-inch MDF with the ¼-inch glass sandwiched between them.

All in all, the project went well. The door fit the jamb and the client was satisfied **(17-44)**. But, there is still something missing in that entry. We'll fix that in the project described in Chapter 18.

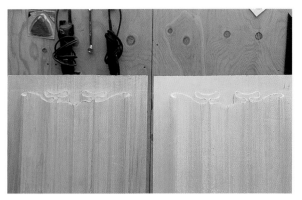

17-44 **Finished panels ready for installation.**

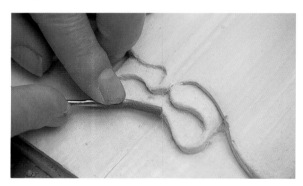

17-43 **Sharp edges are founded slightly.**

17-45 **The panels installed in the door.**

Architectural Carving: Techniques for Power & Hand Tools

UNUSUAL DOOR CASING PROJECT

This project I loved. The finished project would be absolutely unique. There would not be another.

After installing the floral panels and door with panels described in Chapter 17, the homeowners decided that the door casing was far too plain. I couldn't disagree, so I appeared at their door about 6:00 P.M. with all kinds of books and pictures of door treatments. By 11:30 we still hadn't decided on a design.

There was something wrong with every suggestion: too traditional, just like the one at the bank, similar to the one at the old library, and the list went on. These folks wanted something unique.

During our meeting the CD player had been sounding softly in the background, mostly folk music. At one point Joan Baez was singing the folk song "Barbara Allen." I leaned back in my chair and said, "Pretty song."

The lady of the house replied, "Oh yes, it's one of my favo…" I looked at her; she looked at me and we both looked at him.

I smiled and said, "Let's tell a story around your entry."

Let me here quote a few lines from the song:

> She was buried in the old churchyard
> Sweet William's grave was nigh her
> And from his heart grew a red, red rose
> And from her heart a briar
> They grew and they grew o'er the old
>   church wall
> Till they couldn't a grown no higher
> Until they tied a true lover's knot
> The red rose and the briar.

I walked to the entryway and said, "Down here at the bottom we put something to suggest a grave, a plinth block. Then we do foliage up both sides, rose on one side and briar on the other. At the head blocks, we put portraits, William on one side and Barbara on the other. The foliage continues and entwines in the center of the head." Everyone was smiling.

I'll now relate the mechanics of what I did to myself with my big mouth.

THE FACES

It's my way to attack the hard parts first, and the faces were definitely the hard parts for me. I don't have too much trouble with life-size faces in the full round, but these faces for the door treatment posed a little more of a challenge. For them not to protrude excessively from the wall, they would have to be done in high relief. The depth would not be in true proportion. Also, I had to work from photos— but at least we did agree on photos that were taken straight on. I don't think I could carve a tipped face on the first attempt. I admit it. I'm not proud and I'm not all that good with faces. Cherubs with their pudgy faces, wings, and little round bottoms are a lot easier.

After transferring the pattern and cutting the outer edge, I went to work removing waste below the chin (18-1). The drawing/photo is actually a composite of two men, one in his 60s and one in his teens. The reason for this is too long a story to relate. You'll note that there are four nails driven in the blank. These mark the corners of the eyes and the corners of the mouth. When I pull the nails, I will have these points of reference as I carve and I won't have to keep measuring and marking. Also, I have made a cut at the hard line above the eye. This I will also try to keep as I go down. The more points of reference the better.

Why is there a discoloration in the nose area? That is drying cyanoacrylate (CA) adhesive. I intend to add material for the nose. Rather than using viscous CA recommended

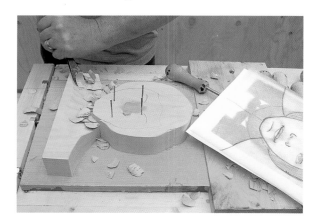

18-1 Waste is removed below the chin.

Architectural Carving: Techniques for Power & Hand Tools

for wood, I use the thinnest. I prime both the blank and the piece to be added with a thin coat of CA. After the prime coat is completely dry—15 minutes or so—I add fresh CA to one piece and exhale on the other; moisture speeds the action of CA. The stick is immediate and the glue line stronger and thinner than with the viscous CA.

After tiring of waste removal beneath the chin, I set in the hairline and began removing waste **(18-2)**. It might seem that it would be better to round off the hair first, but I wanted to keep the sharp hairline as a point of reference as I went down. The area of the hair would also give me a flat reference as I began to round off the forehead.

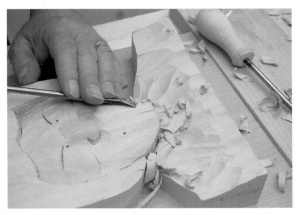

18-3 **The chin and mouth areas are roughed in.**

18-4 **The eyeballs are roughed in.**

187

18-2 **The hairline is set in and waste removed.**

Becoming bored with the forehead, I moved on to the chin and mouth area **(18-3)**. After I was satisfied with the chin for the moment, I began to develop the eyeballs **(18-4)**. You can see that I glued the nose in place and roughed it in slightly. Noticing that the nose was not quite deep enough in relation to the mouth, I deepened it slightly **(18-5)**. I also noticed that the forehead wasn't deep enough and round enough, but material left for the hair was getting in the way. So I gave a little shape to William's "do" **(18-6)**.

18-5 **The mouth area is deepened to make the nose protrude farther.**

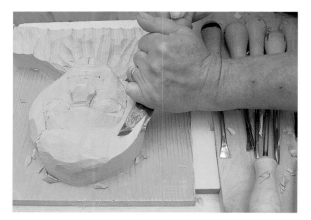

18-6 Shape is given to the hairline.

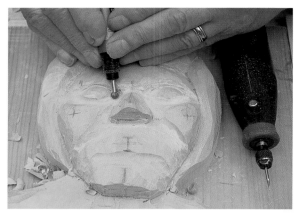

18-7 A burr is used in the difficult area at the corner of the eye.

By this time, you have probably realized that I'm not concentrating on any particular feature, but working the whole face simultaneously. This is the only way I can keep the features in proper proportion in this type of carving. You see, the depth of the features is only about 3/5 scale in relation to the width. I'm taking my measurements from front and profile drawings of the "average" human head and plugging in the peculiarities of the photos I'm working with.

Being satisfied with the general shape of the face and the depth of the characters, I began to define details. There is one spot on a face that I couldn't seem to cut effectively with any kind of carving tool or knife. That's the grain-change area at the corner of the eye. Here I resorted to a burr (18-7). I also used a pointed burr to undercut the area at the base of the nose. While I had the burrs out, I also shaped the rest of the nose and the area where it meets the face.

Before defining the eyelids and mouth, I strengthened the wood in these areas by applying thin CA (18-8). In these areas, there will be some very delicate details. One chip out of an eyelid can ruin it. The CA does seal the wood and can pose challenges with penetrating stain, but most of the sealed area will be cut away, leaving only minor areas that are easily touched up.

18-8 CA is used to strengthen the delicate areas around the eye.

After the CA dried—15 minutes or so—I sketched in the eyelids and began to expose the eyeball. I made stop cuts very gently with gouges, then cut to them with a small skew, removing only a few thousandths of an inch of material at a time. Once the lines were well established I deepened the stop cuts with a knife and began to work a little more boldly (18-9).

By this time I had cut in the hard line between the lips and rounded the lips into it. All that was left was the little smile lines at the corners; these fell to a small skew (18-10). I've found that if the hard line and the rounding of the lips are correct, the outer shape of the lips

Architectural Carving: Techniques for Power & Hand Tools

falls into order automatically. So finishing off the mouth with a medium gouge was easy (18-11). All that was left was that little hollow area from the upper lip to the base of the nose (18-12).

18-9 A knife is used to make stop cuts for the eyelids.

18-10 A small skew is used to make cuts at the corners of the mouth.

18-11 The shape of the mouth is finished off with a medium gouge.

18-12 A tight skew is used to cut the area above the center of the upper lip.

At this point I did a little cleanup with sandpaper and rifflers. If William was intended to be a hard, he-man type, I would have made the cuts more carefully and left the tool marks. But this is "Sweet" William. I saw him with sort of a baby face. Even though he has a basically square and masculine chin, I softened it a bit with sandpaper (18-13).

Nostrils are always a final step for me. If you cut them in prematurely and have to reshape

18-13 The lines of the chin are softened with stiff sandpaper.

189

the nose, you're in trouble. My favorite tool for the task is a burr **(18-14)**.

All that was left was the hair. You'll probably note that all that I had done up to this point was to rough in the hair rather unceremoniously. I took skew in hand and was going to smooth the hair area, then stopped. I only smoothed a couple of very ragged areas. The blocky surface will give the illusion of waves. The illusion of strands of hair became the job of another burr **(18-15)**.

18-14 A round burr is used to define the nostrils.

18-15 A cone-shaped burr is used to define the hair.

The portrait of Barbara Allen was carved with much the same technique. Of course, she being of the opposite gender, the nose was more delicate, and the lips and eyes more—what should I say—inviting. The major differ-

ence was the hair. I had Sweet William all showered, shaved, combed, and dressed in his Sunday-goin'-to-meetin' suit. Barbara turned out to be a bit windblown. I portrayed the hair using a number of different sweeps of gouge and a V tool **(18-16)**.

18-16 The female's hair is defined with a number of tight-sweep gouges.

THE PLINTH BLOCKS

Second hardest were the plinth blocks. I wanted to portray a grave but not an obvious grave. I wanted to avoid such things as gravestones. Guests should ask, "What is this?" Then Joan Baez could go into the CD player, and the host could tell the story. I drew a few sketches but had no idea how I would get what was on the flat paper into a block of wood. I then resorted to a clay model—several as a matter of fact.

I wanted to tip the grave and couldn't quite model it right. Finally, I modeled it in profile. Then I cut both the front and back of the model **(18-17)**. Now I had the grave near a wall as viewed from the foot at a slight angle **(18-18)**, still not quite what I wanted. One more wedge-shaped slice taken from the back, and eureka, there it stood, a grave against a wall viewed from the foot and above **(18-19)**. I wasn't quite sure how I was going to carve the

18-17 The back of the model is cut to establish a different view.

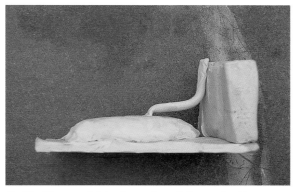

18-18 The model is then viewed from the foot at a slight angle.

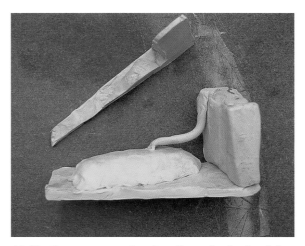

18-19 One more cut is taken from the back of the model to refine the view.

stem of the rose growing from the grave in the model, but I could think about it as I carved the grave.

With trusty model as a constant companion, I began to let in the design (18-20). By this time, I had figured out what to do with the rose; I sketched it in so it could be incise-carved with a tiny burr. The detail would be far too delicate to carve in relief and I wanted the rose to be proportional in size to the grave. After sketching, I textured the "old church wall" before going further (18-21).

18-20 With continual reference to the model, the design is let into the block.

18-21 The wall area of the block is textured before further carving.

The last step of the design was to carve a few lines that would indicate bricks or stone (18-22). I would continue this theme in the casing. To finish up, I carved a mold in the top of the plinth (18-23). Yes, this is a job for a shaper, but it's not worth setting up the machine for a few inches of mold.

Unusual Door Casing Project

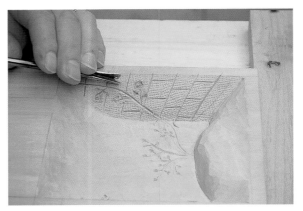

18-22 Lines are carved to represent mortar between bricks or hewn stone.

18-24 A model is used to sketch the design.

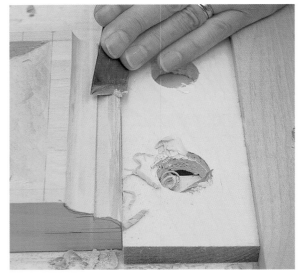

18-23 A mold is carved on the top of the block.

THE CASING

Last but not less challenging came the casing itself. I decided to sketch the design directly on the molded boards. There's no sense in making a pattern to use only once. For the rose, I had a model "borrowed" from a neighbor's fence (18-24). As no one in the neighborhood had a briar growing in his yard, I had to rely on a photocopy from the library.

I decided to do something a little unusual here. Rather than having the design com-pletely captive in the frame of the casing mold, I decided to let a leaf or two hang over the mold. I could glue small pieces on for the extra material needed.

Before risking making mistakes on the molded boards, I decided to do a test carving. I wanted to learn to carve a rose efficiently, and I wanted to see how that overhanging leaf would look. I had carved roses on Victorian-style furniture, but these were only suggestions of roses. I wanted something more realistic, and I wanted the flowers more open than the buds usually seen.

I started by drawing two concentric circles with a small oval in the center, representing petals not yet open. The first thing I did was to set in the oval in the center. This is a very delicate character, so after setting it in lightly, I deepened the stop cut with a burr (18-25). The round burr I used was the same size as the shank. I asked myself, "Do I let the shank ride on the light set-in as it cut deeper and deeper? Perhaps I would carry this stop cut deeper than the background. After sketching in the petals, I realized that the center bud would interfere with the gouge I intended to use for setting in the petals. So I rounded it off and shaped it to resemble a petal that was just unwinding (18-26). Even with that done, I

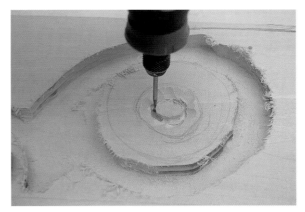

18-25 The stop cut is deepened with a straight burr.

18-27 Stop cuts are made between the petals with a knife.

18-26 A burr is used to make the delicate cut at the center of the bud.

18-28 The faces of the petals is hollowed with a gouge.

had to make stop cuts at the lower end of the petals with a knife **(18-27)**.

After satisfying myself that the petals looked overlapped, I gave them a little extra shape by curling the tips and hollowing out the faces **(18-28)**. It was then a matter of cleaning up the outside of the petals and thinning them a bit **(18-29)**. I actually undercut around the outside and was quite satisfied with the results.

It's not obvious in the photos, but the petal tips lie slightly lower than the tip of the center bud. The outer row of petals, which I will carve in the same manner as the inner, will lie even lower.

18-29 The petals are then thinned.

Finally I set in and hollowed out that escaping leaf (18-30). After standing back for a look, I decided the effect was a definite "keeper"—might even work in an escaping rose or briar flower.

18-30 An experimental leaf, escaping the confines of the frame, is carved.

I won't go on and on with the entire carving of the casing. We have carved enough flowers, leaves, and stems in the foregoing chapters and projects. But I did want to show what was to be unique in this casing.

I had some carving done when I decided to take the pieces to the home and fit them to the jamb before continuing, and it's good that I did. You see the stem leaves Sweet William in an awkward position. The stem that's there will cut away and a new piece glued in at a better location.

As I was about to remove the pieces and return to the studio, the lady of the house informed me that they had a party planned in a few days and asked if I could leave the pieces until after the event. Normally I don't like my work viewed before it's finished, but as I explained earlier, I consider myself a craftsman, not an artist. Then when I was hit with the little dance, the hands in praying position and, "Oh, please, oh, please, oh please," how could I resist. I'm a sucker for a pretty girl.

MAKING THE BEST OF THE SITUATION

If you're asking yourself why the casing begins about ⅓ of the way up the wall, I'll explain breifly as it was explained to me. It seems that the folks that poured the foundation for the home set the bolts on the wrong side of the foundation. As such, rather than a brick veneer, the home was sided with vinyl and the ledge for the brick wound up inside. Rather than fight the ledge I set the casing on top of it.

I did insist on painting the finished pieces and returned them the next day. When I went to tack them in place I had a little problem with driving a nail through Barbara's hair, but I managed. When I came to Sweet William, the best place for a nail was through the throat. I couldn't do it. He is held in place with a few dabs of latex caulking.

18-31 The finished door casing.

194

On my return I did take my camera and snapped a few photos; the most dramatic, I think, was from the top of the spiral staircase across the room (**18-31** and **18-32**).

I also snapped a close-up, because there is one little item that I didn't mention above. Both briars and roses have thorns. I had no intention of carving them as I worked the stem. They would be very delicate, and if I did manage to carve them, they would be easily broken off in cleaning. So rather, I cut small mortises in the stem and inserted small pieces of maple therein. After the glue dried I shaped them into a thorn with a burr (**18-33**).

18-32 **View from the spiral staircase.**

18-33 **Detail of the thorns.**

195

Unusual Door Casing Project

PART IV

USEFUL TOOLS & EQUIPMENT YOU CAN BUILD

19

POWER STROP & SHARPENING STATION

This is a book on carving, not building equipment, but there are some things I consider essential that may be best shop-made. I could work with traditional benches and the like. I started out that way. I've worked that way in other people's shops. But I'm much more efficient and comfortable in my own studio. I've shown you how to build your own workbench in Chapter 1. I will present some more of my ideas on equipment in this and the next two chapters.

This power strop and sharpening station may at first seem a bit of overkill, but I consider it essential in my studio. I really don't think that I could, or would want to, work without it. The machine is portable and I try to keep it only a step or two from where I'm working, and usually it runs continually. Passing a tool over that strop for a mere five seconds can make all the difference in the world.

THE BASE

I've built all kinds of bases for portable tools, but the one I describe here is my favorite. It's heavy enough for stability yet light enough for easy moving while taking up a minimum of floor space.

Start by placing a three-gallon plastic bucket on a piece of plywood that rests on a pair of sawhorses. Both bucket and plywood should have a hole drilled in them to accommodate a piece of ¾-inch pipe. The bucket is a form and can be reused for more bases. The pipe should be threaded on one end to receive a pipe flange—sometimes called a floor flange. The other end should have a hole drilled in it to receive something, such as a large nail, to keep the pipe from turning in the base **(19-1)**. It's also a good idea to plug the pipe below the nail with a wad of paper.

There should be some contrivance beneath the horses to hold the pipe in position, and that position can be checked with a spirit level—sometimes called a "whiskey stick," but since they don't put amber-colored fluid in them anymore, perhaps "vodka stick" is a better term **(19-2)**.

19-2 A spirit level is used to plumb the pipe.

Next, fill the bucket with wet concrete mix. Mix the concrete in accordance with the directions on the bag—don't get it too "soupy." Fill the bucket slowly and tap the sides as you go to purge the concrete of air pockets. Once the concrete is within ½ inch of the top, insert three pieces of plastic pipe about 3 inches long and cut at a 45-degree angle **(19-3)**. Space the

19-1 A large nail is used to prevent the pipe from turning.

19-3 Pieces of plastic pipe are inserted to act as feet.

Power Strop & Sharpening Station

pieces at 120 degrees about the periphery of the bucket. These will act as feet, and using only three, will prevent the base from teetering on an irregular floor.

In about 12 hours the concrete will be set sufficiently that you can remove the bucket gently, but let the concrete cure for about a week before any rough handling.

THE STROP WHEEL

While the concrete is curing, cut three disks: 1¼ inch thick by 6-inch diameter, ¾-inch thick by 3½-inch diameter, and a 5-inch-diameter piece from ¼-inch hardboard or MDF. Glue the two wooden disks together, then bore them in such a way that you can mount them on a motor arbor as shown in the cross section **(19-4)**. Leave the ¼-inch MDF piece separate.

No matter how carefully you cut and bore the disks, they will not be truly round. Mount them on the motor that's either clamped or screwed to your bench, and contrive some sort of tool rest in front of it. A stout, sharp chisel will aid you in truing the disks round **(19-5)**. If you have lathe tools, a bull-nose scraper works better.

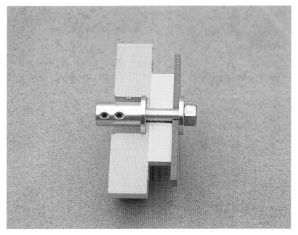

19-4 The disk assembly is bored to accommodate an arbor.

Scrape the edge of the wooden disk flat, and round the corners at a radius of about ¹⁄₁₆ inch. Taper the MDF disk so that it has a radius of about ¹⁄₁₆ inch at the periphery.

Next, prepare a strip of split cowhide that is 1¾-inch wide and 3 inches longer than the circumference of the wheel by cutting one end at a 30-degree angle. Split cowhide is about ³⁄₃₂ inch thick, and the piece you select should be quite firm rather than the pliable stuff that comes from the belly.

19-5 A sharp chisel can be used to true the disks.

200

19-6 The leather is wrapped around the wheel for marking.

Wrap the leather neatly around the wheel and mark the uncut end (19-6). After cutting the leather, spread the face and about ⅜ inch of the side of the wheel with contact cement. Also spread the body side—rough side—of the leather. I strongly recommend two thin coats of contact cement, allowing drying between.

When the contact cement is completely dry, carefully position the leather and wrap it around the wheel. Should the leather begin to go awry, STOP. Squirt some lacquer thinner under it to release the contact cement; then let it dry and try again.

Once the leather is in position, wet about ½ inch of the edges. Wet only the top of the leather; don't get water on the contact cement. Once the water has penetrated for a minute or so, carefully roll the leather over the edge of the wheel (19-7). The water should have made the leather pliable enough that it will compress rather than pleat as it rolls over the edge. As a final step, press the leather firmly against the wheel; the back of a chisel works well for the task (19-8).

19-7 The leather is rolled over the edge of the wheel.

19-8 The leather can be pressed firmly into the contact cement using the back of a chisel.

Power Strop & Sharpening Station

AN ADDITIONAL ACCESSORY

At this point you can mount the motor to a board, then mount that assembly to the pipe flange and thread it onto the base. You may want to add an electrical switch. If you do, don't be tempted to mount it horizontally; brushing by the machine can turn it on accidentally.

Go ahead and screw it on the base, but don't snug it down just yet. Take a few measurements and prepare a 2-inch-by-3-inch piece of wood. From one end measure 2 inches and bore a hole that will snugly accept the pipe. (You'll find that the pipe is $1\frac{1}{16}$ inch in diameter. If you don't have such a bit, there's no law against grinding the edges off of a $1\frac{1}{8}$-inch speed bit for the task. There is also no law against boring a $1\frac{1}{8}$-inch hole and shimming with a piece of veneer.)

Bore two -inch holes at the outer edge of the pipe bore. These will receive two carriage bolts that will clamp the block to the pipe. Take the block to the band saw and make a cut in the center of the block that extends to 1-inch beyond the pipe bore.

Cut the block to length so that a 3-inch caster wheel mounted on it will fall directly below the strop wheel. What you are building is a belt-sanding machine; the strop wheel is the drive and the caster the idler (19-9). Mount the caster by means of a lag screw. (The best type of caster to use is the type with a bronze bushing pressed into the center.) Through this goes a steel bushing that serves as an axle (19-10). And, the axle can be held firmly with the lag screw. On the machine in the photos I used a cheap caster with a phenolic bushing pressed into the center. The bushing actually rides on the lag screw. It would seem that this would not be a long-lasting arrangement, but after putting a drop of oil on the lag, I let the machine run for 12 hours. The caster was a little sloppy, but it was a little sloppy when I first installed it. It was

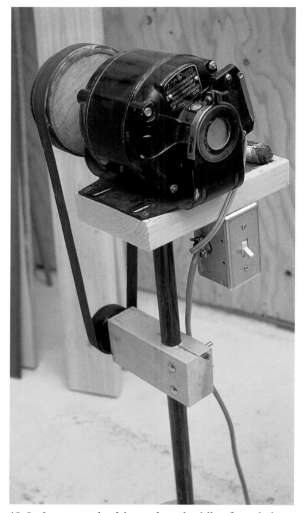

19-9 A caster wheel is used as the idler for a belt sander.

still running fine. (I did stop at three hours and replace the metal washers on both sides of the wheel with snugly fitting, heavy leather washers. I couldn't stand the noise of the steel washers, and the leather does tend to hold oil.)

Once the caster is mounted, hang the belt over the strop wheel and around the caster. Slide the block down the pipe until slack is out of the belt; then tighten the locking bolts slightly. Turn the machine on and check for belt centering. The centering can be adjusted

202

19-10 **A steel bushing is used as this caster wheel's axle.**

by tapping the sides of the block with a hammer to rotate it on the pipe.

If the belt flies off, it's probably not tight enough. Tap the top of the block with a hammer to move it farther down the pipe. In use

the belt shouldn't flop back and forth more than ¼ inch.

After these adjustments are made, you can make one more addition. Attach a piece of wood beneath the motor mount in such a position and angle that it just barely "kisses" the belt **(19-11)**.

THE MACHINE IN USE

In all cases both the sanding belt and strop wheel should run AWAY from the cutting edge. As the sanding belt passes over the strop wheel, it can be used much as a grinder, hollow-cutting the bevel. For a flat bevel, hold the tool against the belt as it passes over the block beneath the motor mount. And for a curved bevel, hold the tool between the strop wheel and the flat block **(19-11)**.

If you are slightly reshaping a tool, use 180-grit belts, then switch to 220- or 320-grit for honing. The scratches left by a 180-grit belt

203

POLISHING COMPOUNDS

There are several types of compound that I've used on the strop wheel. *Emery* is comparatively rather coarse. It can be used to polish out rather deep scratches from tools that have just come from the belt sander. *Jeweler's rouge* is much finer and will put a mirror polish on the tool. I have also occasionally used diamond powder combined with grease. It is a long-lasting abrasive, but should you try it, be sure to use nothing coarser than 600 grit—and use it sparingly.

Apply whatever compound you are using to the wheel while it is stationary. Applying compound while the wheel is turning seems convenient, but most of it will wind up on the floor—try it and you'll see what I mean. Rub the compound generously into the leather, turn the machine on, and go to work.

Can all three compounds be used on the same wheel? Yes, provided you keep in mind what you're doing. If you start with emery, you will notice that it removes scratches from the tool but leaves a rather dull finish. As you continue to use the wheel without reloading it with emery, you will notice that the finish becomes brighter and brighter. What is happening is that the particles of emery are being broken into finer and finer particles. Finally they will become worthless. Emery cuts quickly while it is fresh but deteriorates quickly. For restoring a cutting edge and producing a mirror polish, you'll find that the jeweler's rouge is a fine all-round compound.

One more note: if you apply compound to the face of the disk, it can be used for stropping chisels, skews, and even plane irons.

19-11 A block is used to provide a flat sanding surface.

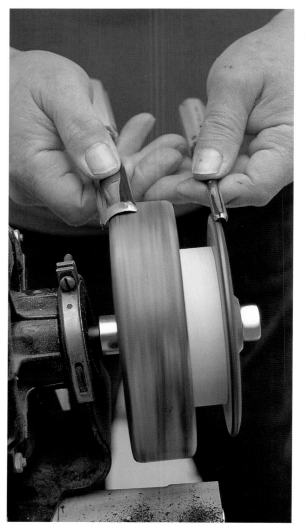

19-12 The corners of the wheel are used to polish the channels of gouges.

take forever to polish out on the strop. The belt is not moving as fast as a grinding wheel, so the prospect of overheating is lessened, but it still exists. Use all the cautions that you would in grinding: frequent cooling and caution at the corners.

Of course, the prime function of this machine is stropping. The face of the leather wheel can be used for the tool's bevel while the corners can be used to polish the chan-

nel of gouges (19-12). The edge of the MDF disk will polish the channels of smaller gouges.

When using the strop, be careful that the point of contact is a little up from the cutting edge (19-13). Keep in mind the resilience of the leather. If it is too close to the cutting edge, the edge will become blunt (19-14). You will know if it's too far from the edge because compound will build up near the edge.

Architectural Carving: Techniques for Power & Hand Tools

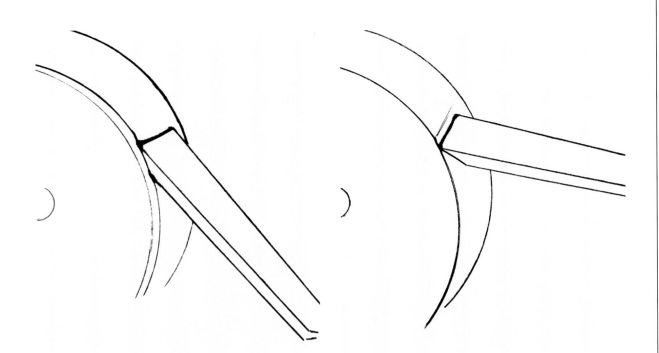

19-13 Proper angle for holding the tool on a leather strop wheel.

19-14 Improper angle: the tool is held too high and will be rounded off.

205

20 HOLDING FIXTURES

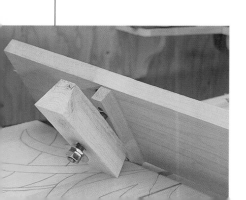

Benches with vises are very handy, but so many times I've found that the vises don't do what I want them to do or do it well enough. Vises are quick and convenient, but with most of the work I do, once I fix a piece to the bench, it's going to be there for a while. A few minutes of setup was not my concern when I built my bench. On the top of my list was serviceability, without things standing beyond the work to interfere with my plan of attack.

FOR BOARDS & PLANKS ON EDGE

One of the first things I used my workbench for was to demonstrate some Southwestern treatment on the edge of a board for this book. This seems simple enough; just clamp the board to the edge of the bench. Putting the clamp on top of the bench wouldn't do; the edge was level with the surface of the bench. The clamp had to go beneath the bench, but this required three hands: one to hold the board, one to hold the clamp, and one to tighten the clamp. (I considered using my teeth to hold the board, but as I get older I realize the value of teeth and was not about to risk them on a board.) I did meet the challenge with a couple of scraps, bored to receive the pipe of the clamp, and a couple of wedges **(20-1)**. This really worked out better than a vise in that I could separate the clamps to accommodate any length of board.

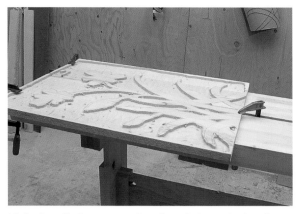

20-2 **Small clamps can be placed through the slot.**

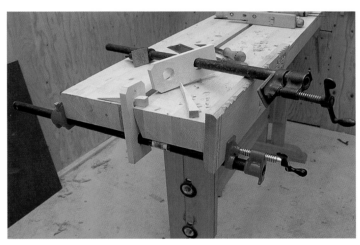

20-1 **Scraps and wedges are used to hold the clamps.**

FOR PANELS

Early on I used the new bench for the "Pair of Carved Panels Project" described in Chapter 15. It was easy to just clamp the panel to the bench. I even found that I could run a clamp through the slot **(20-2)**. Clamps can get in the way and I really wanted something a little more professional looking. So, I drilled three ½-inch holes near the top of a plank and mortised in three nuts on one side. After cutting some slots in the plank to make it height-adjustable, I fastened it to the end of the bench with 6-inch lag bolts **(20-3)**. You'll note two circles on the top of the plank. These are the tops of two ¾-inch dowels that I bored 5 inches into the plank to strengthen it.

I could have run bolts through the holes and nuts, but I have an aversion to snagging myself on things hanging over the edge of the bench. I turned a couple of smooth circles and bored a hole three-fourths of the way through them that was a little smaller than a piece of ½-inch all-thread metal rod. After swabbing the hole with glue, I screwed the all-thread into it.

I calculated that this would be sufficient to hold the disk firmly on the all-thread. Should the glue fail, I would bore a hole from the edge of the disk and through the all-thread. A No. 6 nail then carefully driven into the hole would make things even more secure.

20-3 Lag bolts are used to secure an end fixture.

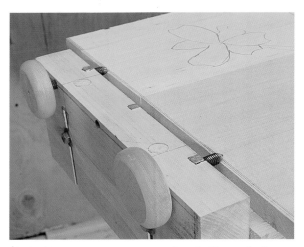

20-5 Clamp screws are tapered to hold panels down.

For the stop, I glued a ¾-inch stick to a 5-inch-wide board as long as the bench is wide. Another piece of ½-inch all-thread through the board, stuck in a piece of dovetailed stock, and the stop stood ready (20-4). You'll note that the edge of the board is ripped at about a 5-degree angle. This will tend to hold the panel down as well as prevent its moving forward. At the vise end you'll also note that I have ground the ends of the all-thread at a taper. This also tends to hold the panel down (20-5). So many times I've found that even when you start with a perfectly flat panel, it will cup as you remove material from the face.

The stop block did prove to be a little thick and interfered with my router on some projects, but it was nothing to shim up the project with a piece of hardboard or plywood (20-6).

FOR MISCELLANEOUS

I can't say that I missed the vises on my old bench. I did a lot of fighting with that vise. Anything that was held had to be held in the center to prevent the vise from twisting. Either that or I had to put a stick the same size as the

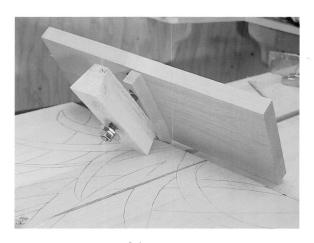

20-4 Components of the stop.

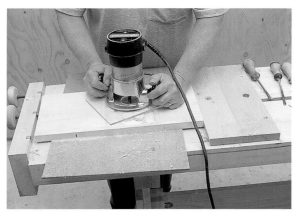

20-6 Panels can be raised to prevent the holding fixtures form interfering with work.

Architectural Carving: Techniques for Power & Hand Tools

item being held on the other side of the vise to balance the pressure.

Any time a vise-type of device was required on my new bench, a "Mogensen" clamp secured to the bench worked just fine (20-7). (Yes, I know that that type of clamp is often referred to as a "Jorgenson" clamp or a wheelwright's clamp, but I bought several of these from a fellow named Swen Mogensen. In my studio they are referred to as Mogensen clamps.)

20-7 A clamp can be used instead of a vise.

The clamp worked just fine, but that one rod hanging so far out became a real pain in the hip. So . . . I secured two "sticks," 2 inches by 2½ inches by about 2 feet long. Through the sticks, I drilled some ½-inch holes to receive ½-inch threaded rod and assorted "goodies" (20-8).

To adjust the rods I again turned some 3-inch knobs from 1-inch material. A 7/16-inch hole—drilled almost through— in the center of the knob let me thread the knob onto the rod after swabbing it with glue. To aid the glue, I drilled a hole through knob and rod to receive a No. 6 finish nail (20-8, lower center).

Before inserting the rods, I elongated the holes along the length of the sticks. (Did I do that by pulling the bit back and forth in the holes? Everybody knows that that is a bad practice. So, I'm bad.) With the elongated holes, the sticks need not be perfectly parallel in use.

Between the knobs and stick there is a shaft collar and a washer. These space the knobs from the stick. On the other side of the stick there is another shaft collar and washer. These prevent the rods from moving through the stick. As the rods pass through the other stick, there is a nut and washer, one on the outside (left) and one on the inside (right). The nut on the left pulls the sticks together, while the one on the right pushes them apart. I found that when using the Mogensen clamp it was best to adjust the center rod the approximate size of the stock then pinch the stock using the outer rod.

I did think of tapping some 1-inch rods and making round nuts and boring them into the sticks much the same as the Mogensen clamp. As I was tapping the first piece of stock I got to thinking that, for quick adjustment, I could spin regular nuts with my finger. The round nuts were set aside.

209

20-8 Components of a shop-made clamp/vise.

Holding Fixtures

To complete the fixture, I padded the jaws with two layers of outdoor carpet, secured using contact cement.

Gentle reader, I must confess that the project was an initial failure. The nuts turned on the washers and it became a three-handed operation to load the clamp. For a time I clamped a pair of locking pliers to the outer nut, but that was very tacky. The whole challenge was met by removing the washers and shallowly mortising the nuts into the sticks (**20-9,** to the right). I will say that the clamp/vise holds some rather large, heavy pieces of stock (**20-9**).

20-9 The clamp/vise in use.

210

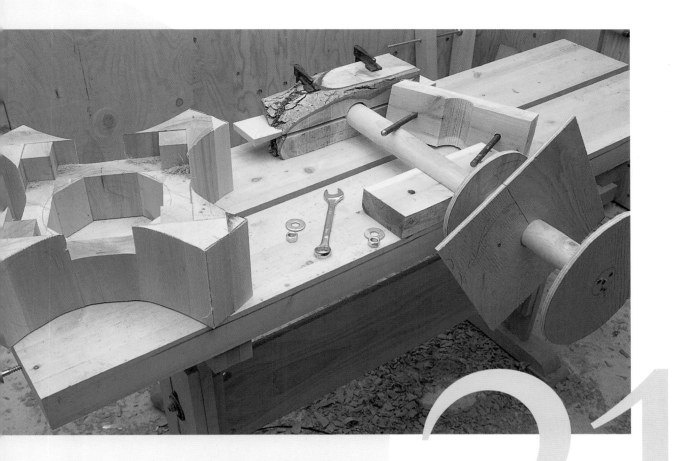

ROTATING DEVICES

I don't think that I could carve in the round without rotating devices. Well, perhaps I could. I did long ago, but I don't think I would want to. I'm spoiled. My first rotating device was actually my lathe. I came up with several contrivances to prevent either the belt or the pulley from moving. The lathe worked fine for small projects, but when I mounted bigger projects and went to work with a mallet, I ruined a ball bearing center. I needed a rotating vise.

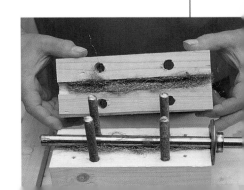

A ROTATING VISE

I came up with a different contrivance for holding things that could be rotated, the components of which are presented in **21-1**. It consists of two blocks of 8/4 material with holes drilled through them about an inch down from the top. Through the block to the right a piece of half-inch threaded rod is inserted. One end of the rod is ground to a taper much the same as a lathe center. On the other end is welded a piece of $\frac{1}{8}$-inch steel. If you don't have the facility for welding, you can drill a hole in the rod and insert a No. 16 common nail. You could clip the end of the nail and peen it over, but you might not have blacksmithing talents. Just wrap a couple of layers of duct tape around the pointed end to keep it from falling out, as I have done with the short piece of rod to the lower right in **21-1**.

On the tapered end of the rod is a nut brazed to a large washer. The washer has a hole drilled in it, and a screw secures the assembly to the block and keeps it from turning **(21-2)**.

Through the hole in the other block goes a piece of $\frac{5}{8}$-..-inch shaft stock. On the end of this goes a spur center, made by drilling four holes in a shaft collar and brazing in pieces of $\frac{1}{8}$-inch drill rod. (There is an in-progress shot of one of these spurs being

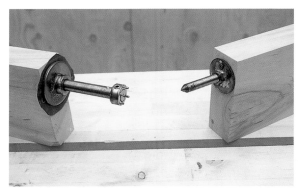

21-2 **The friction washer in position.**

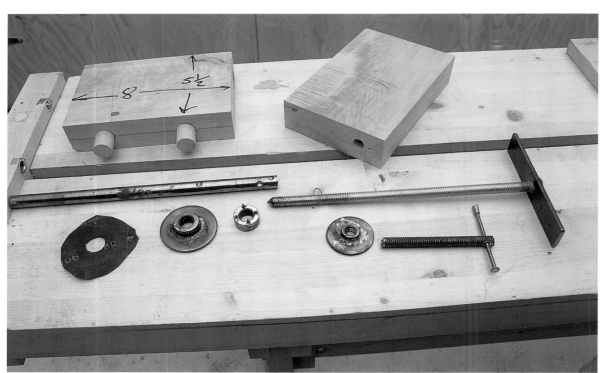

21-1 **Components of a rotating vise.**

Architectural Carving: Techniques for Power & Hand Tools

212

BRAZING

I have mentioned a lot of brazing; if you don't have a torch hot enough for the job, you can substitute solder. There is not a lot of strength required in any of the joints, but do a nice clean job of the soldering **(21-3)**.

21-3 Shaft collar soldered to the friction washer.

used in the deluxe model following.) The ends of the drill rod are sharpened so that they will bite into the stock.

Farther down the shaft is another shaft collar with a large washer brazed to it. This provides friction to keep the stock from rotating freely. To give it even more drag, a piece of rubber cut from an old inner tube is placed between the friction washer and the block. Note the pockmarks drilled into the shaft to aid the set screw of the shaft collars.

If you have a bench with dog holes, bore the blocks and insert dowels to fit the holes, and clamp the blocks to your bench **(21-4)**. Or you can screw the blocks to a stout board and clamp the board to your bench.

This little contraption works very well for small items: balusters, newels, small brackets. I've used it for furniture legs, but found that I had to provide additional support for wing blocks if I did any heavy work on them. Just friction holds stock quite firmly, but there is a danger of unwanted rotation. Try to keep all force perpendicular to the bench and in line with the centers. You'll soon find out what works and what doesn't.

A DELUXE ROTATING VISE

As I mentioned, the small vise above worked well for me on small projects. But now that I had my adjustable-height bench, I was prepared to tackle bigger projects on a rotating vise. A 14-inch-diameter log had been asking me to carve something from it for several years. I had to have a new vise.

The new device was quite a bit huskier but the metal parts remained the same. Rather than clamp it to the bench I ran bolts through the main blocks to hold the dovetail block that slides in the slot in my new bench **(21-5)**. I also decided to make the new device height-adjustable by making self-storing shims to go

21-4 Insert dowels in the blocks to fit the dog holes in your bench.

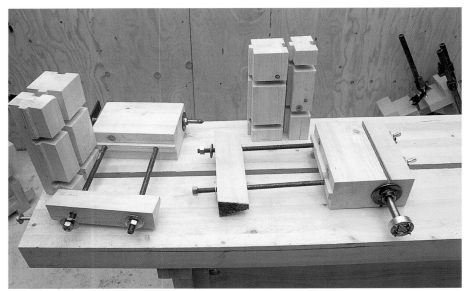

21-5 Components of the deluxe rotating vise.

with it. For stability, I like to keep the centers as close to the bench as the project permits. The self-storing idea came to me through sheer laziness. If I kept shims and blocks all in one pack, I wouldn't have to change the position of the nuts on the rods quite as much. I hate moving a nut several inches up a bolt. I even cut slots in the shims so that I wouldn't have to remove the nuts at all except to mount a main block between the bench supports (21-6).

You'll note the wing nuts on the top of one block. These are attached to bolts that go through the block to secure the top. I should say that they make the top clamp down on the shaft to further prevent it from rotating. The wing nuts adjust the amount of drag on the shaft. I intended to do some work with large stock with this vise, and I felt that just the friction washer would be insufficient.

For the wood stock I glued four 4-foot 2×4s together face to face. After passing the assembly over the jointer to true one face and one edge, I planed it to the thickest I could and still remove the marks of the eased edges of the 2×4s. From this blank I cut the pieces necessary.

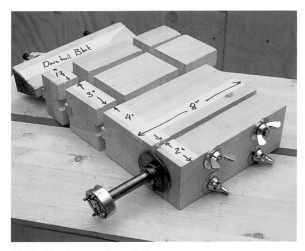

21-6 Blocks are slotted for easy arrangement.

Rather than drill holes through the main blocks for the shaft and threaded adjusting rod, I cut off about 1⅜ inch of the top and ran it over a ½-inch dado for the threaded rod (21-7). To prevent the threaded rod from turning freely, I placed a piece of rubber, cut from an old inner tube, in the slot. After boring holes and mortising in the nuts I inserted the ½-inch mounting rods. Then I fastened the top back in place with drywall screws.

21-7 A dado accommodates the threaded rod.

The rotating end was a slightly different matter. I also cut the top off but ran the dado quite shallow and with a gouge enlarged it to fit the ⅝-inch shaft snugly. The first project I used this vise on was the 14-inch log. I found that I was getting some unwanted rotation even with the wing nuts pulled down with pliers. I pulled the top off the block and lined the slot with coarse steel wool **(21-8)**. That did the trick.

Before cutting the top off the block I drilled it for four ½-inch bolts to clamp the

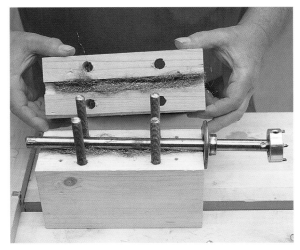

21-8 Coarse steel wool adds friction.

top on with. (I might explain here, why all this ½-inch rod. A friend of mine was working on a project where the plumbers were hanging pipe with ½-inch threaded rod. From each length they used, there was an 18-inch-long piece left over. These the plumbers left for the trash. My friend gathered about 70 of these leftovers and gave them to me. I've been using them for all sorts of projects ever since.)

As I prepared the blocks I was thinking that I would need something a little huskier than that ⅝-inch shaft collar for a center. I purchased a shaft collar that would fit over the smaller one, and soldered in pins **(21-9)**. Just in case that didn't work, I made up another friction-washer-like assembly and drilled holes in it for screws to be used as a faceplate-type device.

21-9 A larger spur center.

And just in case that wasn't big enough, I welded up a three-washer assembly **(21-10)**. (If you weld up such an assembly, feel free to do a better job than I. The only small rod I had that day for my stick welder was one that a friend gave me 15 years ago. Believe me, welding rod, unlike fine wine, does not improve with age.)

21-10 A faceplate assembly.

When I use these faceplates, I drill a ⅝-inch hole about ½ inch deep in the stock and slide it onto the shaft. Then I slide the faceplate up to the stock and insert screws into the stock. If the ends of the stock are not exactly parallel, I don't tighten the screws securely. After securing the lock screw on the shaft, I'm ready for work.

The shaft protrudes about 4 inches from the block. That's to prevent the wing nuts from interfering with any carving I might do on the end of the stock. The other end should also protrude about an inch. This allows me to strike it with a mallet to seat the spur (21-11).

'Tis true that this is a definite abuse of a good mallet, but a steel hammer will tend to mushroom the end of the shaft. Also in **21-11** note the wedge-shaped sticks to hold the stock in place as the spur is being seated.

ANOTHER ROTATING DEVICE

Just about the time I thought I had all of the challenges of carving in the round met with my rotating vise, I was called upon to carve a pair of column capitals. The rotating vise did not have the capacity for the capitals, and even if it had, the bench would not go low enough. Another device was in order.

I decided to mount a shaft on my bench using wooden pillow blocks. The front pillow block I mounted by bolting it to the bench. This necessitated drilling two holes in the new bench and that hurt, but, hopefully, that will be all of the holes I will ever need to drill **(21-12)**. I clamped the rear pillow block and shimmed the halves so that the shaft could turn freely.

What is that dark stuff on the rear pillow block? That is bark; it's found on the outside of

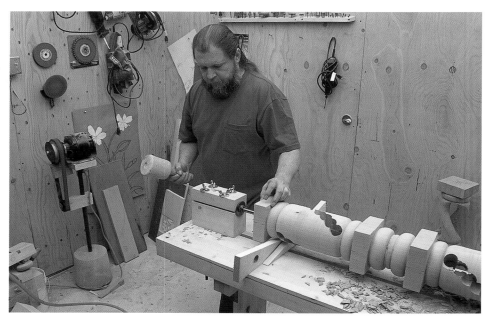

21-11 The spur is seated by striking the shaft.

Architectural Carving: Techniques for Power & Hand Tools

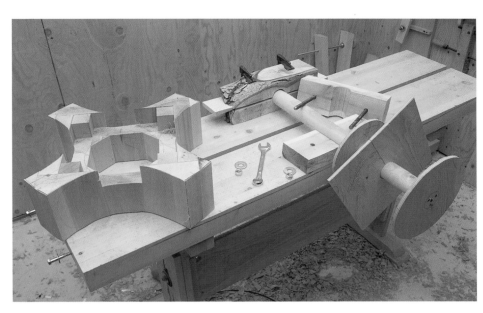

21-12 Holes are drilled in the bench to fasten the pillow block.

trees. You see, I have a friend in the tree-removal business. When I need large pieces of wood I call on my friend. Wedge and hammer or a chain saw begins the process of turning limbs and trunks into lumber. My band saw and jointer finish the process. Yes, the wood is green and it splits and checks as it dries. So what, as long as it remains structurally sound. Above in the section on holding fixtures I described a clamp, and in Chapter 3 under "Routers" I described a router base; both appear to be constructed of what looks like ash. It isn't ash; it's "tree of heaven" (genus *Ailanthus*), fresh cut. In the months that it took to write this book, it shrunk some, but there were no dimensional changes that rendered the fixtures unusable.

To the front of the shaft—which, incidentally, is turned from a fresh tree limb—is screwed a plywood disk that will be screwed to the base of the column capital. Behind the disk is a square piece of plywood that will be screwed to the top. One more plywood disk

serves as a washer to hold the capital away from the bench a little.

Even the square piece—which I cut so that it won't interfere with carving—I fastened to the shaft after they were fastened to the column capital **(21-13)**. How does this contrivance work? You can find out in the "Pair of Column Capitals Project" of Chapter 16.

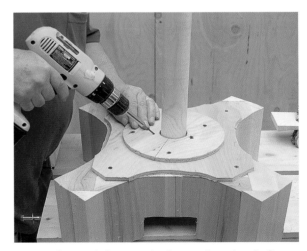

21-13 The work is securely fastened to the shaft.

METRIC EQUIVALENTS
(to the nearest mm, 0.1cm, or 0.001m)

inches	mm	cm	inches	mm	cm
⅛	3	0.3	20	508	50.8
¼	6	0.6	21	533	53.3
⅜	10	1.0	22	559	55.9
½	13	1.3	23	584	58.4
⅝	16	1.6	24	610	61.0
¾	19	1.9	25	635	63.5
⅞	22	2.2	26	660	66.0
1	25	2.5	27	686	68.6
1¼	32	3.2	28	711	71.1
1½	38	3.8	29	737	73.7
1¾	44	4.4	30	762	76.2
2	51	5.1	31	787	78.7
2½	64	6.4	32	813	81.3
3	76	7.6	33	838	83.8
3½	89	8.9	34	864	86.4
4	102	10.2	35	889	88.9
4½	114	11.4	36	914	91.4
5	127	12.7	37	940	94.0
6	152	15.2	38	965	96.5
7	178	17.8	39	991	99.1
8	203	20.3	40	1016	101.6
9	229	22.9	41	1041	104.1
10	254	25.4	42	1067	106.7
11	279	27.9	43	1092	109.2
12	305	30.5	44	1118	111.8
13	330	33.0	45	1143	114.3
14	356	35.6	46	1168	116.8
15	381	38.1	47	1194	119.4
16	406	40.6	48	1219	121.9
17	432	43.2	49	1245	124.5
18	457	45.7	50	1270	127.0
19	483	48.3			

inches	feet	m
12	1	0.305
24	2	0.610
36	3	0.914
48	4	1.219
60	5	1.524
72	6	1.829
84	7	2.134
96	8	2.438
108	9	2.743

CONVERSION FACTORS

1 mm	=	0.039 inch	1 inch	=	25.4 mm	mm	=	millimeter
1 m	=	3.28 feet	1 foot	=	304.8 mm	cm	=	centimeter
1 m^2	=	10.8 square feet	1 square foot	=	0.09 m^2	m	=	meter
						m^2	=	square meter

INDEX

A
Air hammer, pistol-type, 53–54
Alder, wood, 78
Anchoring, 99
Angle grinders, 56–57
Animal figurines, working with, 86–87
Ash, wood, 76–77, 79
Auto-body putty, 129

B
Background
    removal, 115
    texturing, 118, 159
Background texturing, for relief carving, 118
Band saws, 44–46, 98
Bar, carving, 141–144
Basswood, 76
Bead cutting, 170
Belt sander, for sharpening, 73
Benches, 14–17
Bench screw, 16
Bench vise, 16–17, 42, 120, 124, 163,
    208–210
Bent skews, 25
Bevels, sharpening, 61–63
Bit, router, 48–50
Blades, band saw, 46
Boards, on edge, holding fixtures for, 207
Brazing, 213
Burrs, 50–52, 98
Butternut, wood, 76

C
Carbide burrs, 51–52
Carpet pad-knife, 32
Carved Panels Project, 149–159
    buds, 156–159
    cleaning up what router left, 152

door with. *See* Door with Carved
    Panels Project
    flowers, 156–159
    leaves, 154–155
    patching, 151
    pattern development, 150
    setting-in the design, 151
    stems, 153–154
    texturing the ground, 159
Carving machines, 58
Carving tools. *See also specific carving tools*
    acquiring, 26–27
    arrangement of, 13
    expense of, 27
    handles of, 29–31
Cherry, wood, 77
Chip carving
    curved designs, 105–107
    technique, 102–104
    triangular designs, 104
Chisels
    components of, 30
    design of, 23–25
    electrically-powered, 53
    numbering, 28
    pneumatically-powered, 53–54
    socket handle, 30
Clamps, 16, 209
Cleanup work, 152, 154
Color, auto-body putty and, 129
Column Capitals Project, 129, 160–170
    initial work, 160
    setting-in the volute, 162–169
    shaping the blank, 162–169
    working with patterns, 161–162
Corrosive agents, for sharpening, 69–71
Cove plane, shop-built, 179
Curved designs, chip carving, 105–107
Cutting angles, sharpening, 61–63
Cutting edge, 64, 98
Cutting techniques, with band saw, 44–46
Cyanoacrylate (CA) adhesive, 186–187

220

D
Defects, patching, 128–129, 151
Diamond burrs, 52
Die grinder, 52–53, 98
Dimensions, decreasing, 93–94
Dividers, 41–42, 153
Doglegs, 24–25
Dolls, working with, as models, 87
Door Casing Project, Unusual, 185–195
    carving face for, 186–190
    casing, 192–195
    plinth blocks, 190–191
Door knob handle, 30
Door with Carved Panels Project, 129, 171–184
    panel preparation, 177–184
    sash preparation, 172–176
Drawknife, 42
Drivers, 52–53
Dry-brush method, for glazing, 131

E
Efficiency, 13
Emery, 203

F
Faces, carving, 186–190
Files, sharpening, 68–71
Finishing
    patching of defects for, 128–129
    preparation for, 128
    sanding, 129–130
    staining, 130
    strikeout, 132
    topcoats, 130
Fir, 78–79
Floor-covering knife, 32
Floor flange, 199
"Fore-bent" tools, 23–24
Form in the round
    carving, 124–126
    seeing, 125

G
Glazing
    with strikeout, 133
    technique, 130–131
Gloves, 99
Gluing, 79–81
Gouges
    bull-nose, 103
    fore-bent, 23–24
    modifications, 54–56
    power sharpening, 72
    safety precautions, 98–99
    shank design, 23
    sharpening, 62–63
    sweep of, 23
Grain matching, for gluing, 79
Grinders
    safety issues, 72
    for sharpening, 71–73
Ground, texturing, 159
Grounding, 115
Guided scraper, 38

H
Hammer, 34
Handles, of carving tools, 29–31
Hand position, 100
Hand tools, 23–42. *See also specific hand tools*
    numbering, 28–29
    safety precautions, 98–100
    specialty, 25–26
Hard Arkansas stone, 66
Hardwoods, 76–78
Holding fixtures
    bench screw, 16
    for boards & planks on edge, 207
    hold fasts, 16
    for miscellaneous, 208–210
    for panels, 207–208
    toggle clamp, 16
Hollow ground tools, 62
Horseshoe rasp, 35

I
"In channel," 23
Incised carving
    chip carving. *See* Chip carving
    stylized sunflower, 107–112
    triangular designs, 104
India stone, 66

J
Jeweler's rouge, 67, 203
Jorgenson clamp, 209

K
Kerosene, 78
Knives, 31–33
Knots, 78

L
Lacquer, 130
Layout
    decreasing dimensions for, 93–94
    ovals, 89–90
    polygons, 89
    spiral reeds, 94–96
    for spiral shelf supports project, 145
    spirals & volutes, 90–93
    for towel bars project, 136–137
Leaf carving, 139–140
Leaves, carving, 154–155
Lighting, studio, for carving15
Limewood, 76
Linden, wood, 76
Linenfold panels
    preparation of, 177–178
Lubricants, 66–67, 78

M
Macaroni tool, 23
Magnification loupe, 65
Mahogany, wood, 76
Mallets, 33–34
Maple, wood, 77, 79

Measuring devices, 41–42
Metric equivalents, 218–219
Mill glaze, 129
Miter cut irregularity, correction of, 176
Models, working with, 86–87
Muriatic acid, 70

N
Nitrocellulose lacquer, 130

O
Oak, wood, 76, 79
Oil, for sharpening technique, 66–67
Ovals, 89–90

P
Paint roller, for glue spreading, 80–81
Pair of Carved Panels Project. *See* Carved
    Panels Project
Panels, holding fixtures for, 207–208
Parting the twist, for Towel Bars Project, 137
Parting tools, 23
Patching, of defects, 128–129, 151
Patterns
    development, for carved panels, 150
    working with, 85, 161–162
Photography, working with, 85–86
Pine, 78
Planks on edge, holding fixtures for, 207
Plinth blocks, 190–191
Plugs, 144
Pneumatic tools, 52–56
Polishing, 74
Polishing compounds, 203
Polygons, 89
Poplar, 77–78
Power sanders, 57–58
Power Strop & Sharpening Station
    additional accessory, 202–203
    base, 199–200
    machine in use, 203–205
    strop wheel, 200–201

Index

223

Power tools. *See also specific power tools*
    arrangement of, 13–14
    safety precautions, 98
    types of, 44–58
Projects
    carved panels, 149–159
    column capitals, 129, 160–170
    door casing, unusual, 185–195
    door with carved panels, 129, 171–184
    spiral shelf supports, 145–148
    towel bars, 136–144
    workbench, building your own, 16–21
Putty, for patching defects, 129

R
Rabbet, cutting, 173
Rails, cutting, 173
Rasps, 35, 68–71
Relief carving
    applied, 120
    steps in, 114–120
Resins, 78
Retempering, tools, 55
Rifflers, 35–36, 70
Rotating devices
    another device, 216–217
    vises, 212–216
Round, carving in
    holding the form, 124–126
    spiral reeds, 123–124
Router
    bits, 48–50
    for relief carving, 115–116
    types of, 47–49

S
Safety precautions, 98–100
    band saw, 46
    dull router bits and, 50
    with grinders, 72
    during sharpening, 69, 70
Sanders, power, 57–58

Sandpaper, 40
Sash, door, 172–176
Saws, 26, 44–46, 98
Scorp, 42
Scrapers, 36–38
Scratches, on tools, 63
Sculpting device, 57
Setting-in the design, 151
Sharpening. *See also* Power strop and
      sharpening station
    bevels, 61–63
    cutting angles, 61–63
    files, 68–69
    lubricants for, 66–67
    power systems for, 71–74
    rasps, 68–69
    rifflers, 70
    safety and, 69, 70
    of scrapers, 36–38
    steel burrs, 68–69
    stones/devices for, 66–67
    techniques, 60–74
    tool shape and, 65–66
    V tool, 67–68
Sharpness of tools
    factors affecting, 60–61
    testing for, 64–65
Sheffield List
    tool catalogue numbers, 28
Shoe rasp, 35
Skewed gouge, 25–26
Slide projectors, 86
Socket chisel, 30
Softwoods, 78–79
Solvent-based chemical coatings, 130
Spiral reeds, carving, 94–96, 123–124
Spirals, 90–93
Spiral Shelf Supports Project, 145–148
Spokeshaves, 42
Spoons, 24
Spring dividers, 42
Spring joint, 80

Staining, 130
Stains, glazing, 130–131
Steel burrs
    sharpening, 68–71
    types of, 50–51
Steel bushing, 202
Stones
    cleaning, 67
    sharpening, 66
Strikeout
    with glazing, 133
    technique, 132
Stropping
    power, 74. *See also* Power Strop
        & Sharpening Station
    technique, 67, 74
Strop wheel, 200–201
Studio, setup for, 13–15
Surfacing putty, 129

T
Template
    design, 93–94
    for router, 48
Texturing the ground, 159
Texturing tools, 33
Toggle clamp, 16
Tool catalogue numbers, 28
Tool marks, sanding, 129–130
Tools. *See also specific tools*
    hardness, 60–61
    retempering, 55
    shape, 65–66
    sharpness, 60–61, 64–65
Topcoats, 130
Towel Bars Project, 136–144
Triangular designs, chip carving, 104

Twist, for Towel Bars Project,
    carving, 138–139
    parting, 137

U
Unusual Door Casing. *See* Door Casing
    Project, Unusual

V
Varnish, 130
Veiners, 23
Vise
    bench, 16–17, 42, 120, 124, 163, 208–210
    rotating, 212–217
Vodka stick, 199
Volutes
    layout for, 90–93
    setting-in, 162–169
V tools
    for chip carving, 103–104, 106–107
    new, sharpening of, 67–68

W
Walnut, wood, 77
Water, for softening wood, 79
Wheelwright's clamp, 209
Woods for carving
    buying, 20
    hardwoods, 76–78
    softwoods, 78–79
Workbench, building your own, 16–21
    center support, 20
    final assembly, 20
    legs, 19
    material preparation, 17–18
    top, 18
Workbenches, 14–17

Index